The Academy of Golf at PGA National

PLAY BETTER

GOLF

FOR SENIORS

THIS IS A CARLTON BOOK

This edition published in 1998

Text © Mike Adams, T.J. Tomasi with Kathryn Maloney, 1998
Design © Carlton Books Limited 1998

A CIP catalogue record for this book
is available from the British Library.

ISBN 1 85868 444 7

Project Editor: Julian Flanders
Designer: Tony Truscott
Production: Garry Lewis

Printed and bound in Dubai

Note: For convenience of presentation, we have presented the material in this book for right-handed golfers. Obviously, the mechanics of the golf swing will apply to all senior golfers.

PICTURE CREDITS

The publishers would like to thank the following sources for their kind permission to reproduce the pictures in this book:

All photographs Warren Raatz, except:
Jeff R.Ackerly 19, 146, 150b, 153l
Marc Feldman 8, 22l, 105-7, 108t, 112, 151, 153r, 155
Kathryn Maloney 9, 103-4, 113
Terry Renna 15, 18
Tony Roberts 10
Sargent & Associates: 6, 48, 60, 72, 78, 114, 117, 118, 122l, 134, 138b, 144, 147
Senior Golfer Magazine 84, 89, 92-3, 95/Tony Roberts 86, 87, 90-1
Visions in Golf/Mark Newcombe 97

Every effort has been made to acknowledge correctly and contact the source and/copyright holder of each picture, and Carlton Books Limited apologises for any unintentional errors or omissions which will be corrected in future editions of this book.

The Academy of Golf at PGA National

PLAY BETTER

GOLF

FOR SENIORS

MIKE ADAMS & T.J. TOMASI
WITH KATHRYN MALONEY

CARLTON

Graham Marsh is one of the best senior players in the world.

Contents

Jack Nicklaus – Golfer of the Century.

You have heard the phrase a thousand times: "Golf – the game of a lifetime." But, as you age, this game you were supposed to enjoy for a lifetime seems to take on a whole new face. No one needs to be reminded about how the aging process changes our physical condition, but it is obvious you are not the same person you were when you were 30 or 40 years of age. Fortunately, one of aging's more gracious gifts is wisdom, and wisdom dictates that as your body changes, so must your golf swing.

This book is dedicated to showing senior golfers, or those fast approaching the age of wisdom, how you can adapt your swing, your playing strategy, and even your mental approach to accommodate your changing body. We don't believe in the saying that you can't teach an old dog new tricks.

Research in learning has proven you really are never too old to learn. Armed with the knowledge of how to adjust, you can make your senior game healthier, more enjoyable and, most importantly, competitive.

The first step in the learning process is to accept your changing body and realize that, if your game isn't what it used to be, it's not your fault! As your body changes you must make adaptations to your golf swing. Senior golfers who struggle with a golf swing more suitable to their sons and daughters are forcing themselves to stay with a swing that just doesn't fit any more. Without some adaptation, their golf swing is like an old suit outgrown by its owner.

So there comes a time when you should switch swings, and this should be done knowingly, using a detailed blueprint of the Senior Swing. The question is, how do you know when it is time to switch? You'll know that it is time for a change when:

■ your in-swing posture changes as you struggle to get the club up and over you, or around behind you,

■ your ball flight becomes erratic and you lose distance,

■ you feel like you're playing old golf as the young lions knock the ball 50 yards past you off the tee,

■ you have aches and pains in the morning that you didn't use to have,

■ you get tired on the last few holes,

■ you find yourself riding in a cart more than you used to,

■ you have trouble seeing the ball land,

■ your touch and ability to judge distances eludes you for long stretches of time,

■ you're consistently missing more greens and getting the ball up and down fewer times than you used to,

■ your scoring range widens so much that you can't tell within 15 strokes what you might shoot on any given day,

■ on your good days, you feel and play like your younger self, but, on your bad days, it's the worst it has ever been.

The upshot of all these symptoms is that your body and swing no longer match. The solution is to coordinate the two, so they can work in harmony once again.

Our revolutionary concept of the Senior Swing offers you a blueprint for modifying your swing to match your body's current capabilities. The bottom line message of this book is that you can put some sand back in the hour glass – if you know how!

The principles of the "Senior Swing"

As you get older, your body undergoes some significant changes. Loss of strength and flexibility, increase or decrease in weight and weight distribution, less mobility, poorer eyesight and slower reflexes are all part of the aging process. However, exactly when and in what combination these changes occur is a very individual thing, depending in a fairly large part on factors such as heredity, the environment where you live, work and play, your diet, your mental attitude, and your personal habits, like regular exercise.

As these changes become apparent, some compensatory adjustments must be made if you are to continue playing an enjoyable game of golf. During the years you played your best, your swing mechanics suited the way your body was put together. Granted the match may not have been perfect – few are, in truth – but it was good enough to play a reasonable game. Now, since your body has changed, you need to adjust your swing by addressing the following topics: your set-up fundamentals, your swing, your short game, the equipment you play with and your course management and strategy skills.

In this book, you will find comprehensive plans for making these adjustments. We will also offer examples from the Senior Tour, including those great players who have continued their world-class play, and others whose playing ability has risen a level relative to their age group. We believe these seniors have sustained or increased their competitive skills by adapting to meet the changes age has brought to their bodies.

You will find extensive information about how to choose the right equipment, how to increase or maintain your fitness, healthy choices for maximizing your potential, and a guide to compensating for the more serious physical problems that come with aging. Regardless of your playing level, from expert to beginner, you'll find the material in this book a breath of fresh air because all of the information is customized to your needs as an advanced golfer (in years that is).

A match to GO

In Chapters 1 and 2 we outline the set-up fundamentals, and the specifics of the Senior Swing which are designed to give you a powerful model for repairing the mis-match between your body and your swing. Without swing adjustments for aging, the mind is willing but the body is not. When you give your body a task it isn't physically able to carry out, your scores will sky-rocket. But when your body and swing match, you create a comfortable situation where you get a GO signal.

With an achievable goal in mind, you can make a sound golf swing, because you are now physically capable of doing so. The most frustrating thing in golf is to get a NO signal while you are standing over your shot because your mind realizes that your body is incapable of carrying out the order.

To avoid NOs and produce GOs you need

to structure your golf swing around your current physical ability so that your swing mechanics fit the characteristics of your body, like flexibility and strength. To do this, you'll learn the set-up keys and the swing mechanics of the Senior Swing, which are adaptations of those old standards you probably learned in your youth. The idea is to consider the problems you are facing as your body changes and offer solutions by adjusting your set-up and swing to maximize your strengths and minimize your weaknesses. We haven't found the golf swing version of the fountain of youth, but in a sense these adaptations allow you to hit the ball more like you did in your younger years.

The rest of the story

But there's more to maximizing your strengths and minimizing your weaknesses than adaptations to your swing and set-up. You will learn how to adjust your swing to the specific physical problems you may face as a senior. Hip replacements, arthritis, shoulder problems, and even bifocals can all take their toll on your game. Though we

don't pretend to offer miracles, we can show you how to compensate for these problems in your golf swing so you can play to the best of your potential.

You will learn score-saving shots around the green, with those fundamentals and techniques relevant to the more "advanced" golfer. If your game has changed, so should your strategy. How do you deal with going from being a long hitter to a shorter hitter? If you are an aggressive player, is there another way to attack a golf course other than overwhelming it with fire-power? We will show you the strategies and mental techniques that you can apply in order to revitalize your game.

Next, your clubs need to be fitted to your body and your swing. With all of these fundamentals in order, you have freedom to match your shot selection on the course to your own strength and weakness profile, which is a realistic assessment that custom fits your game to the golf course layout. With this powerful, comprehensive approach, everything is in place to allow you to play better golf as a senior.

Hogan speaks

In an interview with *Golf Digest* editor-in-chief Nick Seitz, Ben Hogan was asked if he ever considered playing the Senior Tour. "No," said Hogan, "I always considered myself a junior." Next, Seitz asked Hogan what he thought of the Senior Tour players: "The older ones, it seems to me, have done away with the back swing and the follow through" replied Hogan.

Though it is understandable that one of the greatest players in history – the greatest ball-striker of all time – didn't wish to display a lesser swing or a lesser game, Hogan's answers touch on a sentiment that can be damaging to seniors struggling with the game they love. Trying to hold on to your junior swing will cause you endless frustration and may take the joy out of the game. Or worse, you may give up the game entirely. Hogan's observation about the seniors' swings hits the nail on the head. Though Hogan, a purist, didn't like the abbreviated look of the seniors' swing, he seemed to know that this is what it took for his contemporaries to continue playing at a competitive level.

Hogan's choice is understandable. He had achieved greatness and, after a near-fatal car accident which was supposed to have ended his career, he returned and dominated the game with even greater skills. Later he chose to leave competitive golf entirely and said he was happy with his choice. Having fought and won such a courageous battle against great adversity, it is no wonder that Hogan was content to retire.

But we hope you will continue in golf, continue to learn and improve, continue to be competitive and, most important of all, continue to enjoy the game, without being thwarted at every step by the aging process. The purpose of this book is to help you achieve that goal.

Chapter one

The five fundamentals of the set-up

A great advantage golf offers over other sports is that you can prepare yourself perfectly for every shot you play, just as well as an expert would – if you know how. This preparation phase is known as your pre-shot routine, which you will learn about in later chapters. But the core of the routine is in the details of your set-up: how you hold the club, aim the club-face, and arrange your body in relation to the target and the ball.

The choice is yours: set-up correctly so you capitalize on the ability to prepare for every shot, or make set-up errors and unwittingly prepare for failure. When you set-up to the ball correctly, your chances of making a good swing dramatically increase. For every set-up error you commit, you will have to make a compensating move during your swing if you are to hit the ball well. Every golfer, regardless of age, has the ability to set to maximize their current potential for the best possible golf swing and golf shot.

We estimate that improper set-ups cause over 90 percent of swing errors. For example, if you aim too far to the right of the target, you have to flip your hands over at impact to hook the ball, or spin your chest and pull the ball back on target. Either way, you introduce one mistake as compensation for another, and you can't play your best golf with a

Like all great players, Senior PGA Tour star David Graham knows that golf's great advantage is being able to prepare fully for every shot you play by setting-up correctly.

patchwork quilt of errors that will unravel at the least provocation.

In this chapter you will find the details of the Senior Swing set-up that is designed to maximize your strengths and minimize your weaknesses. If you have been playing golf for a long time, you will find the details simply an adjustment to the standards you learned years ago. We understand that no one likes to make changes, but the instant results you will find will quickly make you forget the uncomfortable feelings change can cause. A good rule to follow is "don't confuse comfort with correct."

If you are new to golf, you will be able to build your swing from a foundation that is designed specifically for your current needs, not the needs of a 30-year-old. As a beginner you should be particularly diligent about your set-up when you practice. This way you will ingrain the correct swing mechanics as quickly as possible and keep the inevitable bad shots to an absolute minimum.

The no-excuses set-up

While of utmost importance, a correct set-up doesn't require much athletic ability. Unless you have a physical disability, there is no excuse for an incorrect set-up. Every golfer can be as perfect as Jack Nicklaus or Hale Irwin, at least at address. And the more meticulous you are about your set-up, the closer you are to perfecting your swing. Using the guidelines that follow ensure you set up every swing for success.

The grip

Where the
Vs are

Another way to check your grip is to look at the Vs, the shapes that are formed on each hand where your thumb and hand pinch together. For the senior grip, the V of your left hand should be pointing at your right shoulder and the V of your neutral right hand should point to the right side of your face.

Since your hands are your only connection to the club, and therefore to the ball, one of the most important fundamentals of a good set-up is having a correct grip. The function of the grip is threefold:

■ to establish and maintain control of the club-face,

■ to allow the proper cocking of your wrists,

■ to create a link between your body and the club.

For senior golfers, we recommend the use of a stronger left hand grip position (that is with the left hand rotated clockwise away from target, more on top of the handle) and a neutral right hand grip position (right palm facing target). This configuration allows you to maximize your wrist cock and helps you to create extension in your back-swing by swinging the club-head in a wide arc. In the chapter on the full swing (Chapter 2), you will learn all the benefits of the senior power-grip.

1 With the shaft vertical, place your left hand on the club so the pad of flesh at the heel of your hand is on top of the grip, and your thumb is extended.

2 When your grip is correct, the heel pad of your left hand will be on top of the club.

Your left hand grip

To take up the grip correctly, hold the club in front of you in your right hand with the head up and the shaft perpendicular to the ground. Lay the club handle across the base of the palm of your left hand (where your fingers join your hand). Close your fingers and fully extend your thumb down the grip. The club should be anchored under the heel pad (not the thumb pad) of your left hand,

allowing firm control of the club without inducing tension. With the club anchored, you will be able to relax your arms and shoulders, which maximizes the cocking and un-cocking of your wrists throughout the swing. Also, because you aren't squeezing the club to death, your relaxed muscles can move quickly, producing maximum club-head speed and so increasing your power.

When your left hand grip is complete, you will find that your wrist joint (where the two tendons of your left thumb form a small pocket) is slightly to the right of the top of the club handle. This strong grip position will maximize the natural releasing action of the club-face through impact.

Your right hand grip

When you add your right hand to the grip, especially if your chest is large, hold the club in front of you rather than with the club-head resting on the ground. Your right hand simply comes in from the side with the palm facing in the direction of the target. Your goal with your right hand is a finger-grip that joins your right palm to your left. To do this, place the grip along the middle segments of your fingers. A common mistake at this point is to position the grip too much in the palm of the right hand by grabbing the underside of the grip with the right palm. Overlap your right pinkie (little finger) onto

3 Be sure to place your left thumb between the channel formed between the thumb pad and heel pad of your right hand.

4 When your grip is correct you will have a firm hold on the club without tension in your arms and hands.

The interlock
and ten-finger grip

There are three possible grip variations depending on how you place the pinkie of your right hand on the club. The choice is a matter of taste; all three are equally "correct." For the "overlap grip," the right pinkie overlaps your left index finger. For the "interlock grip," the right pinkie weaves between the left index and left middle fingers, meeting around the knuckle so the club rests more in the fingers rather than in the palms. If you choose the interlock grip, do not weave your fingers so deeply that the bases of your palms touch. This forces the club too high into the palms, preventing correct cocking of the wrists.

For the "ten-finger," or base-ball grip, all fingers are on the club, with the right pinkie finger snug against the left index finger. The ten-finger grip can be effective if you have limited strength, inflexible wrists, or any other problem that makes it hard for you to cock your wrists. Choosing a grip is a matter of personal preference but regardless of the grip you use, be sure it satisfies the check points for a good grip outlined here.

The grip *continued*

the area between your left index and middle finger. With your fingers set around the bottom of the grip, join your right palm to your left hand so that the channel between the thumb pad and heel pad of your right hand accommodates your left thumb. When your right hand is closed on the club, your thumb and index finger should form a trigger with your right thumb positioned slightly to the left of the top of the club.

Once both hands are on the club, check the position of your right hand by extending your right index finger down the shaft. If your finger extends down the side of the shaft, your right hand grip is correct. If it extends on top of the grip or on the underside of the grip, your grip is incorrect.

Now try an experiment. Move the club up and down in a hammering motion. If your grip is correct, you should be able to do this simply by cocking and un-cocking your wrists. The club will feel light and your arms should feel relaxed. If the club feels heavy, or your arms have to help your wrists move the club up and down, then the club is too much in the palm of your left hand.

Grip pressure

Checking your grip pressure is an important part of a good set-up. If you squeeze the club too tightly, you cannot cock your wrists the way you should. This denies you leverage, the power source created when your left arm and the club shaft form a 90-degree angle during the back-swing. If you grip the club too lightly, your brain will sense it and at some point in your swing, you will have to re-grip to maintain control – and the last thing you need during your downswing is a sudden burst of pressure that tears the club-head out of its track.

Now, it is true that the "effective" weight of your club changes as the speed of the club-head increases during the swing. It is also true that grip pressure increases when this happens, but this is a gradual build up of pressure and the adjustment will occur automatically if your grip is correct. All you have to do is start with the correct grip and the right grip pressure, and your brain will take care of the rest without you having to think about it.

Your goal is to hold the club exerting equal pressure with both hands. It is hard to describe in words exactly how much force you should use. Suffice to say that your grip pressure should be firm enough to control the weight of the club, but not so tight that movement is restricted. For special situations like hitting out of heavy rough, you will grip the club more firmly, but on a scale of one to ten, where ten is very tight, your grip pressure for normal shots should be about a five. Start with the least amount of pressure then increase it to the maximum. Relax your hands again until you find this middle ground.

Posture

They say the eyes are the first thing to go, but what matters more for senior golfers is the early loss of flexibility. Unlike strength, which diminishes gradually over time, loss of flexibility starts even before the senior years and tends to accelerate rapidly. In Chapter 8 on fitness, you will learn how to slow this process down and even regain some suppleness, but some loss of flexibility is something you have to accept and make adjustments for in your swing. This is one reason we recommend that seniors use a golf posture where the spine angle is more inclined toward the ground.

Bending from the hips

Regardless of age, your body is designed to bend forward from the hips rather than from the waist. When you bend from your hips, your spine tilts but it doesn't curve. Not only is this good for your golf swing, it is good for your back as well. When you bend from your waist, you hunch your back and lock your hip joints, which restricts your hip turn and makes you slide your hips laterally more than you should during the swing, a

3 When your posture is too upright your chest blocks your arm swing.

1 Correct golf posture is established by bending from the hips so your arms can swing freely across your chest.

2 Your posture is correct when you can swing your left arm 45 degrees across your chest.

15

Posture *continued*

If you have been bending from your waist up to now, try the following drill to develop a feel for bending from the hips during your set-up. Your back will certainly thank you for it.

With your knees straight (not locked), place a shaft across your hips, parallel to the ground. Now push the shaft backwards until your rear end protrudes and your weight moves to your toes. Then flex your knees slightly until your weight is redistributed from the balls of your feet back to your heels.

movement that robs you of power and can hurt your back. The good news is that, like many swing errors, you can correct it with the right set-up fundamentals, in this case good golf posture.

By bending correctly from your hip joints, you also create room for your arms to swing. This is especially important for seniors for several reasons. First, if you are like most seniors, you will have become a lot less

The correct knee flex keeps your lower leg almost vertical and your knees over the balls of your feet.

flexible and this shortens the amount your arms can swing. When you bend from the hips rather than the waist, your arms hang freely without the tension in your neck and shoulders that restricts your arm-swing. Second, many seniors are a bit thicker through the mid-section than they once were, and bending over more removes any obstacles that may be in the way of the arms. Third, the senior posture facilitates a more upright swing plane, the benefits of which are outlined later on.

To establish good posture, take your grip as described above, and stand erect with your left arm on top of, rather than beside, your chest. With your arms hanging comfortably from your shoulders and the club shaft held horizontal to the ground, simply let the club-head drop to the ground as you bend forward from your hip sockets. Don't make the mistake of tucking in your tail or you will ruin your posture. When you are in correct golf posture for the Senior Swing, you will have just a slight amount of knee flex and your rear end will stick out behind you.

To be sure you have bent over enough, let your left arm swing across your chest. You should have created enough room for your left arm to swing at least 45 degrees across your chest, the position it will be in at the end of your take-away. If your arm runs into your chest before it reaches 45 degrees, just bend over a bit more until you can swing without interference from your chest.

Knee flex

Since the senior posture requires that you bend over more, your club-head is closer to the ground than it would be if you were more upright, so you won't need much knee flex.

Regardless of the amount of hip bend, you never want to flex your knees in a way that moves them closer to the ball. You will need some knee flex for mobility but remember that your knees are designed to bend your body backward, not forward. This means that your lower leg should be straight up and down and your knees should flex just a little bit until you feel your weight has been evenly distributed from the balls of your feet to your heels. Whatever happens, please do not squat with your knees jutting out over your toes.

Head posture

Your head should be positioned in the middle of your shoulders, not tilted to one side or the other, with your chin up and off your chest in a natural position. If you tuck your chin in tight to your chest, you will dramatically restrict your shoulder turn and ruin your power-coil, an error that a senior golfer cannot afford.

If you tuck your chin in because you wear bifocals, be sure to see Chapter 3 on physical problems to learn how to cope with this.

Once you've taken your address position, you can check to see if you are the correct distance from the ball as follows. Take your right hand off the club and spread your fingers. You should be able to pass your spread right hand between your left hand and your body. If there is room for more than one hand, you are reaching too much for the ball. That puts the weight out on your toes and leaves you in an unbalanced position that feels powerful but, in fact, is not. If your hand cannot pass through this gap, you are too close to the ball, with an excess of weight on your heels. The correct position is when your hands hang about one hand-length from the front of your left thigh, with your weight distributed from the balls of your feet back to your heels.

Teeing height

Be sure to tee the ball at the proper height. A driver should be teed so that half of the ball is above the top edge of the driver when the sole of the club is on the ground. Irons should be teed rather closer to the ground. A good rule of thumb for irons is to tee your ball so that only the thin end of a tee fits between your ball and the ground. If you tee your irons too high, you run the risk of hitting the ball high on the club-face, and because you've missed the sweet spot, your shot won't go as far as you planned. When you tee your woods too high, you could literally skim right under the ball and contact the top of the club-head rather than the face. This error produces a very high, short shot affectionately known as a "pop up," as well as tell-tale scratches on the club-head.

Ball position

Correct ball position is a prerequisite for solid contact because the ball's location affects both your shoulder alignment and the steepness of your swing. If the golf ball is too far forward in your stance (toward the target), you will have to turn your chest toward the target in order to sole the club-head behind the ball. This "opens" your shoulders and, because the club naturally swings along the line of the shoulders, you will be stuck with an out-to-in slicer's swing path. This also means that your body literally blocks your back-swing, adding an unnecessary restriction that is especially destructive to the senior player.

For seniors we recommend that you play the ball further back than the standard "junior" position. As you are probably starting to notice, each element of the senior set-up is designed to match the other elements. As a unit, these adjustments will improve the mechanics of your full swing. Playing the ball back in your stance allows you to use a strong left hand grip to maximize the power of the natural release of the club at impact. With the ball forward and a strong grip, you will hit a vicious hook, but with the ball position correctly matched to the strong grip, you will hit a powerful draw. As you will learn in the next sections of this chapter, this ball position also compliments the closed stance recommended for the Senior Swing.

For medium to short irons, position the ball in the center of your stance. For long irons (which we hope you don't have) and utility woods (which we hope you do have) position the ball one ball-width forward of

Ball position varies depending on what club you're using.

the center of your stance; for the driver and other woods off a tee, the position is two ball-widths forward.

The foot fault

Whether you are aware of it or not, the flare of your feet can distort your ability to judge the ball's position within your stance. Try the following experiment. Stand with your toes pointing directly in front of you and the ball in the center of your stance, opposite the mid-line of your body. Now flare your left foot toward the target; the ball appears further back in your stance. Return your left foot to square and flare your right foot away from the target; the ball appears to move forward in your stance.

Don't be fooled

To avoid letting this illusion damage your set-up we recommend that you check ball position using upper body references. When the ball is supposed to be in the middle of your stance, verify its position by checking it is also opposite your nose or the center of your chest. For long irons and utility woods, where the position is one ball-width further forward, the ball should be opposite the left side of your face. For the driver and other teed woods, the ball should be opposite the middle of the left side of your chest, where a logo would be if your shirt has one.

1 When the ball is too far forward in your stance, your arms will lift off your chest and the club will start back well outside the target line. This causes a steep, out-to-in swing that very frequently results in a weak slice.

2 By positioning the ball back in your stance you will free your arms to swing and match the other elements of the senior set-up and swing.

Stance width and foot flare

Stance width

The width of your stance influences your stability, balance and mobility. Stance width is measured from the inside of your heels. Seniors should use a wider-than-standard stance. This accommodates the lateral upper body motion the senior player uses in the

full swing to generate power. But you should be careful that you do not overdo this, or you will find that you quickly reach the point of diminishing returns.

For the driver and other woods off a tee, your stance will be at its widest, with the inside edges of your feet beneath the outside edges of your shoulders. You should progressively narrow your stance as you use shorter clubs, but your full stance should never be narrower than the inside of your feet beneath the outside edges of your hips.

The knee check

To check that your stance width is correct, take the widest stance as recommended above and turn back and then forward to your follow-through position. If your right knee just about reaches the back of your left knee, your stance is correct. If there is a gap, your stance is too wide. If your right knee passes your left, your stance is too narrow.

Foot flare

To increase your ability to turn back and through the ball, flare each foot between 25 and 45 degrees at address, depending on your flexibility. The left foot should be flared toward the target and the right foot flared away from the target. This is also another way that you can offset the effect of decreased flexibility and add mobility to

Seniors should use a wider stance for stability, balance and greater mobility.

1 When your feet are flared you have a greater ability to turn your hips.

2 When your feet are square, your hip turn is restricted.

both your upper and your lower body.

The amount of hip and shoulder rotation you can achieve during your back-swing depends on your level of flexibility. The less flexible you are, the more a flared right foot will allow you to turn behind the ball. As you will see in the swing section, an over-the-top move is allowed in the Senior Swing, but it

certainly is not a large scale over-the-top move that cuts across the ball at impact. A flared right foot will help you keep this move in check and allow you to approach the target line from the inside. When your left foot is flared out at address it is easier to rotate your left hip and knee correctly as you swing through the hitting zone.

21

Aim and alignment

The term "square" is often used but rarely explained, so in each of our books and all of our schools we use the following description. To understand this key concept, lay down four clubs as follows: one along the target line; one along your foot line parallel to the target line; one club from your left heel perpendicular to the target line; and one from your right heel also perpendicular to the target line. The four clubs form a square. Your feet, knees, hips, and your shoulders are "square" when they are parallel with the target line, as is your club-face when it is perpendicular to the target line. Making this square with your clubs on the ground clearly shows the geometric relationship between your body, the club-face, the ball, and the target line.

Aim and alignment are both defined in terms of the target line, an imaginary line connecting the target to the ball.

Aim refers to the direction your club-face points in relation to the target line. When it looks to the left it is called closed, when it points to the right it is open, and when it looks directly at the target, the club-face is deemed "square."

Alignment, on the other hand, always refers to the direction your body faces. When it looks to the left of the target line it is open, to the right it is closed, and when the imaginary lines connecting your shoulders, hips, and feet are all parallel to the target line, you have a square body alignment.

We believe that you can pre-set your body alignment at the address stage to encourage the position you want to achieve at the top of your swing. The ideal position at the top is when your body is coiled (that is, when your shoulders have turned more than your hips) and your weight has shifted over to your right side.

When you were a "junior" player you probably learned to aim your club-face at the target and align your body just left of the target line but parallel to it. But as flexibility decreases, a square position can limit your turn, and, what matters most, your coil.

> The club-face is "square" to the target line when the bottom edge of the club is perpendicular to the line.

Therefore, while your club-face must aim at the target, you should arrange your shoulders and hips in a slightly closed position, by pointing them directly at the target itself instead of parallel to the target line. This pre-sets your top-of-swing position and is as much a part of a good senior shoulder and hip turn as the motion itself.

The next step in the pre-set is to drop your right foot back from parallel to the target line, so your stance is closed. The line of your toes now points directly at the target rather than being parallel to the target line. Some words of caution here: As you make these two adjustments, be careful not to disturb the square position of your club-face – it must stay aimed at the target.

With the club-face aimed at the target, a closed stance gives the less flexible senior player greater ability to turn behind the ball.

The final element in the pre-set is weight distribution. Since your weight must shift to your right side during your back-swing, pre-set some there at address to make sure it is over your right hip by the time you reach the top of your swing. When the ball is teed for your driver and three wood, your weight distribution should favor your right side by about 70 percent to 30 percent, and with the rest of your clubs by about 60 percent on your right side at the start. However, remember that weight distribution from the front of the feet to the back is another story. Your weight in this sense should be spread evenly from the balls of your feet to your heels, with the majority of it focused on the inside edges of your feet.

A good set-up blends together

It is easy to see how each of these modified set-up fundamentals is dependent on the others and it is important to realize how they compliment each other and combine to match the adjustments necessary in the Senior Swing. For example, the stronger grip matches a ball position that is further back in your stance because it means that the club-face reaches impact before it begins to close in relationship to the target line. These two modifications blend perfectly with a closed body alignment to produce a powerful shot that starts slightly right of the target and curves back to it.

Since it is the club-face that makes contact with the ball, its position and path at impact obviously determine the direction the golf ball travels. It is helpful to use the vertical lines on the club-face (that form a square with the grooves) for aiming. It may sound simplistic, but you must take great care to aim your club-face at the target and position

Aim and alignment *continued*

the ball back in your stance as we have explained. This is the blend that starts the ball to the right and must be matched with the grip that brings it drawing back to target.

The alignment of your hips is a key part of the blend because your hips dictate the amount of rotation away from, and back to, the ball. Open hips at address restrict the back-swing and cause your hips to open too early in the downswing. Since the stance we

A square stance is standard but it can severely limit an inflexible person's ability to turn behind the ball.

recommend is closed, your hips will be closed as well, which allows them a greater degree of rotation in the back-swing.

Each element of the set-up depends on the other elements being correct in order to work effectively. Basically, your set-up is like a chain, no stronger than its weakest link. When each element is correct they will all blend together to form a powerful, solid foundation for the Senior Swing.

A closed stance allows your arms to swing easily across your chest, increases your ability to turn, and directs the club on the proper path in the takeaway.

Chapter two

The senior swing

Swing back, not up

Arnold Palmer, the King.

If you have reduced flexibility, you will have difficulty swinging the club high above your body without straightening your spine. If you try to swing the club up and over you, like Davis Love or Fred Couples, you will pass the limits of your flexibility and tilt toward the target at the top of your swing. This position causes a reverse weight shift, giving you a tell-tale "fire and fall back" finish.

It is just as bad when you swing the club behind you. Once again, because of a lack of flexibility (especially if you have a generous mid-section or large chest), the club gets trapped, meaning that you won't get it back in front of your body in time for impact. This error can cause an over-the-top move in which you are forced to throw the club-head across the target line, to impact far too steeply. This produces a variety of mis-hits, especially pulls, slices and fat shots.

A reverse weight shift occurs when a golfer pivots on the left hip in the back-swing (see below) and the right hip in the down-swing, just the reverse of what should occur. This error commonly causes a variety of fat and thin shots. If you are lucky enough to make clean contact on occasion, you will hit weak slices because it also causes an out-to-in swing path. With the power of your weight moving away from the ball, the reverse is one of the greatest power-robbing swing errors in all of golf. As a senior you can avoid this error by letting your head float over your right foot in the back-swing to make sure that you've loaded up your right side. From there it is much easier to get to your left side during the down-swing.

In this chapter we'll show you the alternative that the Senior Swing (hereafter known as the S swing) offers. The crux of the S swing is to decrease the emphasis on a high arm movement, and focus on moving the club away from your chest as you turn during the back-swing. With the S swing, you swing the club away from your body by pushing with your hands. This moves your body behind the ball while keeping the club and your hands in front of your chest. The S swing enhances your ability to coil with

1 One way a less flexible player forces the club to parallel is by collapsing his left arm break down.

2 If you try to swing the club past your level of flexibility your spine straightens and your golf posture is destroyed.

maximum wrist cock so that the mass of your body is behind the ball at impact. Most importantly, it gives a direct route to the ball in the down-swing, ensuring solid, powerful contact as a result.

Three keys for the S swing

The moving coil

How does the S swing produce distance? The key is the "moving coil" method, coupled with the principle of "low hands, high club-head." The moving coil means your upper body moves laterally as you turn, allowing you to swing your left shoulder behind the ball as your right hip turns over your right heel. It is not, however, a sway because your weight stays on the inside of your right foot and your right hip turns instead of sliding.

The head leaves its address position when it is allowed to follow the movement of the upper body in the back-swing.

Low hands, high club-head

In the set-up chapter you learned to hold the club with a strong left hand grip and a long left thumb, a combination that maximizes wrist cock. This is a vital power element because your shortened swing means your hands and arms stay low to preserve your posture and coil, but your club-head swings on as high an arc as possible due to the large amount of wrist set. By using the low-hands-high-club-head move, you take advantage of three power sources: the club-head arc, the leverage created between your wrists and left forearm, and, of course, the power your muscles contribute.

The direct radius

How does the S swing produce accuracy? By using the "direct radius" method. This means that your hands are on a straight line with your chest throughout the swing, and you establish the most direct route to the ball, one that will produce a consistent, repeatable impact position.

With these essential concepts coupled with the particulars of your set-up that you learned in the previous chapter, you are now ready to learn the S swing.

The S swing in detail

The fundamentals you learned in the set-up chapter set the stage for you to draw the ball, a powerful ball flight that starts right of the target and curves no more than about ten yards back to the target. For a senior who wants to regain distance, learning to hit a draw is imperative. If you have survived with a slice so far, now is the time to learn to draw the ball because that slice is destined to get shorter, weaker and more crooked.

Pieces for learning

Though we would never want you to think of a swing in "pieces" when you actually play the game, we have separated out various swing stages so we can describe them in detail and clarify every element. Keep in mind that while sectioning a swing into pieces is contrary to the overall concept of a golf swing, it can be helpful as a format for explanation. Once you've learned the details though, banish these pieces from your swing thoughts. Call upon the pieces only when you are having trouble with your swing and have time to go to the driving range to work on whatever element is causing the problem. To master your swing you will blend all the individual parts into a rhythmic motion known as the golf swing.

Address

As you learned last chapter, you begin the S swing from a slightly closed address position where your club-face aims at the

Once you've mastered the S swing we are certain you will hit the ball better than you have in years. But even the best swings in the world can go off track now and then. The question always is, how do I get it back? We strongly suggest that you avoid tinkering with any mid-swing elements and start with the basics.

Take your book and go to a full-length mirror. Open to the set-up chapter and use the photos and the mirror as a guide. Has your left hand grip slipped from strong to neutral? This is the most common mistake, and an easy one to make. Is your posture too erect, or is the ball too far forward? If you find the problem in your set-up, and chances are you will, make the adjustment and then hit some balls to reintroduce it to your swing. Remember, every error will cause another, so give the rest of your swing time to adjust to your new set-up.

If the problem wasn't in your set-up, no doubt you will find it early in your back-swing. Follow the same process, giving your entire swing time to adjust to the correction.

Address *continued*

target as usual, but your body also points at the target itself, rather than parallel left of it, which is the usual prescription. Remember that the corresponding ball position for the S swing is back of the standard. If you adopt the other elements of the S swing and set-up, but neglect to move the ball back, you will hit pull hooks that go a long way, but are hard to find. By employing the new standards you learned in the set-up chapter, you will establish your posture by bending more from your hips so you have sufficient room for your arms to swing across your chest rather than simply picking the club up without coiling.

The take-away

The take-away only lasts an instant but it is critical to the overall quality of your golf swing. To get off on the right track, use a one-piece take-away where your hands, arms, chest and the club all move away from the ball as a unit. To guide you in the initial path of your swing, use an extension of the line established by your toes. Your hands should follow this line and the rest of the members of the one-piece unit should maintain the relative positions they held at address as they move. But be careful not to force the club-head straight back along the target line. Instead, as your stance is closed, you should let it swing back inside the target line as your hands move along your toe line.

To visualize the one-piece take-away, think of a triangle where your arms serve as the sides and your chest forms the back of the triangle. The club-shaft extends down from the point of this triangle like a spire on a church steeple. As your hands travel over your right foot, the triangle moves away from the target intact, with all relationships between its faces remaining constant.

The head float

Although there should be no conscious effort to move your head during the swing, forget advice you have heard about keeping your head still. Let it move as part of the one-piece unit. Even the youngest, most supple players, like Tiger Woods, Ernie Els and Phil Mickelson, let their heads move behind the ball during the back-swing. It's a subtle move but it is a part of every good swing. Older players, and/or those with less flexibility, let their head float even more and so should you. Just make sure that you don't overdo and force your right hip to slide outside your right heel. In order for your head to move correctly, keep your neck and shoulders relaxed. If they are tight, you will freeze your head in its address position and your only option will be to lift the club to the top of the swing without coiling. This destroys your golf posture and your swing.

You should be aware of your weight moving to your right leg as you start your take-away because the mass of your body is moving behind the ball, and your hips are turning in response to the motion. Even if you are firmly inflexible, when you get to this point in the swing your left foot should be firmly planted on the ground. You may let it rise later in the back-swing, but if it is up at this point, you will inevitably lose coil and ruin your swing-path.

The take-away ends when your hands are just past your right foot. As the take-away blends into the back-swing, the heel pad of your left hand pushes down on the handle to set your wrists, elevating the club-head without you actually needing to raise your arms. Once you move away from the "pieces" of your swing and blend them into one motion, a hint of this feeling will occur almost immediately as your club leaves the address position.

Understanding "let"

Throughout this chapter you will see various references to "let" this or that happen. Make no mistake about our choice of words here. For example, the advice to "let your head move behind the ball," does not mean you should force your head toward your right shoulder. Instead, "let" means that the action is not a result of conscious manipulation on your part – it occurs as a result of some other action in your golf swing. You let your head move behind the ball because the turning of your body naturally pulls it in that direction. So be careful to interpret the word "let" as something you allow to happen rather than actively "make" happen.

1 A common error in the take-away occurs when the left arm rolls out from the chest and breaks the powerful connection between arms and body.

2 When the hands act independently they often ruin the take-away by rolling the club-face open.

The back-swing

The complete back-swing motion is a combination of arm swing and body turn, where your arms do the up and down, and your body does the around. Note that, while the arms swing up and down, you don't force them high for power. You let them swing up as your body turns until you reach your threshold of flexibility, at which point, you are at full coil. For the flexible person, this will result in a higher hand position than for one with less flexibility, and this is as it should be, given the differences in physical characteristics from golfer to golfer.

As these motions occur, your left shoulder moves behind the ball and the pressure of your weight transfers onto your right hip joint. Once again, we've separated out each motion to describe it in detail but, to work effectively, you know they must be blended into one, seamless motion.

Even though your arms and hands swing up, we would like your concept to be that they swing back and away from you. This way you won't try to lift the club, trying for a high arc. If we could give every senior only one piece of swing advice, we would tell you

to repeat the following mantra before every swing, "it's a back-swing, not an up-swing," meaning that the club swings away from the ball and the up part takes care of itself – if you let it. This is good advice for a player at any age, but an especially wise doctrine for the less supple golfer and, if you are a senior, it is an absolute swing saver.

So the concept, the hallmark of the S swing, is that your body, mostly your upper half, turns behind the ball with no effort to get the club high above you. In other words, the arms swing as high as they will, not as high as they can.

If you have been playing golf for many years, you know that your club-head has to create enough arc for power, so you are probably wondering how you will arrive at a happy medium, somewhere in between too long and too short a swing. Though your hands stay lower than they do in a standard swing, you will set your wrists aggressively in the back-swing. This creates sufficient height and length of arc. Whatever arc you lose to a shorter swing, you will gain by swinging the club wide away from you in both your back-swing and your down-swing.

Low hands, high club-head

As you make the transition from take-away to back-swing, you begin to set your wrists as your left shoulder continues its turn behind the ball. Your goal is to keep your hands low but set the club-head high. This way you take full advantage of the powerful leverage your wrists provide. A good thought to achieve full cocking is "low hands, high club-head'. To accomplish this goal, push down on the grip with the heel pad of your left hand while your right palm applies pressure to your left thumb. This cocks your wrists correctly to their maximum.

Using this motion to cock your wrists also helps turn your body behind the ball. The pressure exerted by the right palm serves to pull your left shoulder behind the ball and also protects you from trapping the club behind your body. Pushing the club away from you prevents your left arm from collapsing. A wide swing, where your club-head is kept away from the body, is the key to power, and to keep your swing wide, you should maintain a sense of pushing the club away from you throughout your swing. Remember, if you are pushing down with the heel pad of your left hand, and out with the palm of your right, you will never have to worry about your swing getting too narrow. It is physically impossible to exert pressure away from you as described and collapse the club into your body at the same time.

So this push/set wrist action increases the gap between your hands and your chest, creating the widest and highest possible swing arc for your flexibility profile. This is a key to the S swing for several reasons:

Wrist cock produces a lever which, if saved for impact, multiplies your strength and club-head speed. It is the same concept as using a long pole to move a big rock: the lever, in this case the pole, is the multiplier. With the lever multiplying your strength, the boulder is easily moved; without the multiplier, you don't have enough strength even to budge the boulder.

The back-swing *continued*

■ it creates the maximum swing arc while keeping your posture intact,

■ it helps move your body behind the ball for power,

■ it positions the club on a direct route to the ball for solid contact,

■ it satisfies the leverage requirement necessary to multiply club-head speed.

As the back-swing unfolds, you will feel your weight move onto your right hip joint. This now establishes your right hip as the point of rotation. In your down-swing, the process will reverse itself and your weight will move to your left hip joint, which is the point around which you will find that you rotate through impact.

During the back-swing, it is perfectly alright if your left heel comes off the ground. In fact, if you are very inflexible, it is a necessity. The important point is that you let your left heel rise, as necessary, only when it is pulled off the ground by the tug of your upper body. This way you'll retain your coil while you turn.

1 To learn the "push/set" wrist action characteristic of the S swing, use the split-hand grip drill. Leaving your left hand at the top of the grip, move your right hand down to the end of the grip. The left hand can easily push down on the handle while the right hand pushes the handle away.

2 The split-hand grip drill teaches the "push/set" wrist action and ensures that the hands stay low while the club-head achieves maximum height and width.

Top of the swing

At the top of the swing, the correct position for your right forearm is related to your flexibility and the size of your chest. Large-chested, players with low-flexibility respond to the unique wrist cock of the S swing by angling their right forearm toward the target line as the right elbow folds. This in turn produces what's known as a flying right elbow, a position where the right elbow is well away from your side at the top of the swing. If need be, the senior player who can't use other "high swing tactics" can use the flying right elbow. It fits perfectly with the other mechanics of the S swing and gives the club-head a bit more height.

Because your grip is strong, the flying right elbow also keeps the club-face from getting too closed (facing the sky) at the top of your swing. When you fly it, your right forearm slants at the same angle as your spine with the shaft pointing to the sky. If you do fly the elbow, you should expect less of a draw.

The back-swing is completed when your left shoulder is behind the ball, your wrists are fully cocked, and your weight is about 80 to 90 percent in your right hip socket. Folding your right elbow rather than lifting your arms elevates the club to its final height at the top of your swing.

When your back-swing is complete, you should feel that your left arm is parallel to the ground. Although momentum will take your arm higher than you think it is, left-arm-parallel is a key feeling that keeps your arm swing under control. This will be the hardest feeling to become accustomed to simply because it is hard to go from a long swing to a short one. Your brain thinks that height is power. When you first try shorter swings, you will be tempted to jump at the

Top of the swing *continued*

ball to make up for what you perceive to be a loss of power. But in time, if you trust the concept, you will stop lunging.

At the top of your swing, the club is short of parallel, in a square or even a slightly

> Coil is produced when your shoulders turn further than your hips.

closed position (angled a bit toward the sky). Your left arm is extended away from your body and the club is in front of your chest rather than behind your right shoulder. Both wrists are cupped because of your strong left, weak right grip. If you have good flexibility, your right elbow will be bent so that your right forearm and upper arm form a 90-degree angle. If you are less flexible, the angle will be less, but never less than 45 degrees. For all players, the right forearm should be angled to the ground at the same angle as your spine.

Your shoulders should turn about twice as much as your hips. This sets your body in a coiled position that translates into power when you unwind it in the down-swing. Standard instruction calls for about a 90-degree shoulder turn and a 45-degree hip turn, producing the coil mentioned above. But remember that coil is simply a ratio. If you can't turn your hips 90 degrees – and many seniors can't – it is not a problem. All you need to do is turn your shoulders more than your hips to create the proper ratio. For instance, if you can only turn your hips 40 degrees, you can create the proper ratio by turning your shoulders 80 degrees. In this case, you would ruin your swing struggling for the standard 90-degree turn your body can no longer achieve. The point is, whether your ratio is 80/40, or 90/45, the result will remain the same: your muscles stretch to power your swing.

The down-swing

The pro slot

In a standard swing played from a square stance, there is a shift-then-turn down-swing sequence, where the weight shifts from the right hip to the left hip and then the body turns to bring the club to the ball. The senior swing has a turn-then-shift sequence where the upper body turn occurs first, as part of the re-set. This puts the club between the body line and the target line, a channel called the pro-slot where the club-head is then delivered to the ball from inside the target line. Once the club is re-set in that channel, the weight shift occurs. Simultaneously, the right elbow tucks back in to your side. When this happens, the right elbow is in front of, or at least even with, your right hip, a position necessary to keep the club on the correct inside approach path.

Re-set then tuck

Since your stance is closed to account for limited flexibility, you don't want to drop the club to the inside as the initial move in your down-swing. In the S swing, you move your right shoulder out toward the target line enough to re-set the club to a position between the toe line and the target line. Then your weight shifts, your right elbow tucks and you are ready to turn your hips

through the hitting zone. This is not, however, the classic over-the-top error since the club-head comes onto the target line from the inside, rather than across it from the outside on a slicer's path.

In the case of the S swing, the club is re-routed out toward the target line by the upper body turn where the right shoulder and hands move together for an instant. From a square stance this move would create a swing path where the club-head comes to

37

The down-swing *continued*

In a good golf swing you will use three axes: your spine, around which your upper body moves, and your left and right hip joints, around which, each in their turn, your entire body rotates. While you are swinging, your goal is to have pressure on the correct hip socket at the correct time.

To establish a hip joint as a center of rotation, you shift your weight onto it and then turn your body around it. Remember, your hip must be over its corresponding heel in order for the hip to rotate correctly while you swing. When your club head is moving away from the ball, the weight should be flowing into your right hip joint. When your club head is moving toward the target, pressure should be flowing into your left hip joint. Even though the third axis of rotation, the spine, moves in the S swing, it still serves as the axis of rotation for your upper body turn, which is why it is known as the "moving coil."

the ball from outside the target line, side-swiping the ball. This would produce one of three ball flights: a slice, if your club-face is open to this path; a pull if your club-face is square to this path; or a pull-hook if your club-face is closed to this path. But because your stance is closed, and your set-up is arranged to accommodate the re-set, the

The human body is equipped with powerful levers, multipliers of power, that can be an integral part of your swing if used correctly. This leverage is produced by cocking and un-cocking your wrists and bending your right elbow to create a 90-degree angle between your left arm and club-shaft. Unfortunately, your club can also be elevated by lifting your arms or straightening your spine. This produces minimal coil, and the various benefits of leverage are substantially reduced. Cocking your wrists and bending your right elbow elevates the club and allows you to maintain your spine angle and your arms-to-body connection.

1 From a square stance, an over-the-top move creates a path where the club-head is forced outside the target line and then across it in the down-swing.

2 The senior player is allowed a slight over-the-top move, but, since the stance is closed, the club-head still approaches the ball from inside the target line.

club-head stays off the target line because the right elbow tucks into your right side.

Note that large-chested players, who have a tendency to fly the right elbow because of limited flexibility, still must tuck it back to the right side until it is even with the right hip. But they do it later than those with smaller chest size/greater flexibility, who are not as much closed at address. However, large or small, flexible or not, both types must tuck the elbow to return the club-shaft at impact to the angle it had at address – a universal prerequisite for hitting good golf shots. This move separates the good S swing

player from the poor one. When the poor player comes over-the-top, there's no elbow tuck, and this leaves the elbow trapped outside the right hip. The result blocks the club-head from the necessary inside path, and causes an out-to-in swing path that produces a slice.

Once the re-set is complete, the weight shifts onto the left hip, making it the axis of the down-swing. The S swing now becomes a right-sided swing, a hitting action where the right side provides the power by pushing the club to the ball in a powerful "shoveling" action as the body twirls around the left hip.

Impact

As you can now see now, the key in the geometry of the S swing is the closed stance, so that even though you swing the club-head over your body line, you are still approaching impact from the inside. Done correctly, and with a good release of the club, this action produces a powerful draw that adds yards to your shots.

The release for the S swing allows no breaking down of the left hand. The forearms rotate in response to the momentum of the club-head so the release is full with the club-head turning toe-over-heel. This gives the S swing a "slashing arms" look because the arms release the club-head around the body. When the re-set is exaggerated, there is evidence of a blocking action where the left forearm rotation is held to a minimum. This produces a chicken wing position of the left arm, where the left elbow juts out toward the target in an effort to keep the club-face on line longer. Unless you are very strong, this action is not recommended.

During the down-swing, your head and

your swing center (located just below the throat) float back again to the original address position, then stop to let the arms swing by. This, and hitting the left wall, are responsible for the passive release of the club-head. Both heels face the ground until after impact. The right ankle rolls to the inside during the down-swing which keeps the right heel from flipping out toward the target line.

Full release

Just past impact both arms are straight for the only time in the golf swing because of the straightening of the right arm through the hitting area. Continued body rotation, combined with the force of momentum, then causes the right forearm to pass over the left so that the butt of the golf club slants toward the target line.

Impact *continued*

The finish

The head release

The finish should be erect with no bowing of the body because the club travels more "around" the body with your shoulders level to the ground. In the S swing, the head must release early after impact, much like Annika Sorenstam of the LPGA Tour, Brad Faxon of the PGA Tour or Jim Colbert, a Senior Tour star. This encourages you to keep everything rotating through the hitting zone, and it is also easier on your neck and back. The early

head release allows you be become upright (the "I" position) much sooner, protecting your back from the damaging "Reverse C" that has ruined so many golf games. Players like Ian Woosnam, Jim Albus and Arnold Palmer finish in the "I" as do bad-backers like Rocco Mediate and George Archer.

Note that while early release gives the appearance of the head coming up and off the ball before impact, it actually does not; it releases after impact as part of the full body release as the body swivels up into the finish.

Summary of the S swing

Your S swing is cued by an upper body move away from the ball, that begins with a one piece take-away and ends in a push-down/ push-away cocking action of the hands. The left shoulder moves behind the ball as the weight shifts to the right hip. The head does not remain fixed. Instead, to allow the player to get behind the ball, there is a slight float or drift of the head as the coil is completed. Since the upper body is in control, the S swing looks more arms-orientated, with the lower body functioning as a base for stability and balance. The swing is short, with low hands, but wide as the club-head travels away from the body with the hands in the middle of the chest. The club-shaft is a bit steeper going back than it is coming down because the tucking of the right elbow during the down-swing shallows out the swing arc. The power comes from a full release of the forearms and body through the ball, a release that causes the ball to start slightly right and then draw back to target. The body is straight at the finish with 100 percent of the weight on the left side and the club horizontal to the ground.

Using a long-shafted driver

If you are like most senior golfers, you've probably lost some yards off the tee and have thought about getting, or already own, a long-shafted driver with a jumbo head. You will learn all about the dynamics of these clubs in the equipment chapter but, all else being equal, a longer club swings the head on a larger arc and this translates into greater swing speed and longer drives. In addition, the larger head gives you an expanded hitting surface and a more forgiving sweet spot that increases the odds of making solid contact, another essential for long drives.

It is an interesting combination that even the young professionals are taking a close look at. Senior Tour player Rocky Thompson, once considered a short hitter, is now one of the longest hitters out there after switching to a 52-inch driver (that's a bit much for most of us). Gary Player, at 60-plus, is hitting his new bomber further than he drove it in his prime.

But while both the physics of the golf swing and actual experiments by expert players tell us this is more than just the latest golf equipment hype, there are some

adjustments you need to make to your S swing if you are going to benefit from a long-shafted, big-headed driver.

To accommodate the increased length of the club shaft, you will need to stand taller at address. The senior player needs to bend more from the hips at address, so this can be a problem. Solve it by decreasing your knee flex and making sure you place your left arm on top of your chest, rather than dangling to the side. Because of the added length, you stand farther away from the ball and this means your swing will be more rounded.

You already have a wider-than-normal stance, so you don't have to adjust your foot-width, but you should flare your right foot a bit to allow the club to swing comfortably around you during your back-swing. You should also modify your normal weight distribution at address. Instead of 70 percent on your right foot, pre-set 80 percent there. Take care to keep the weight on the inside rim of your right foot, distributed from the ball of the foot back through your heels. This will give you a stable platform to hit off as you swing the long driver.

Using a long-shafted driver *continued*

When you are focusing on hitting the ball farther, be careful you don't increase your grip pressure too much in anticipation of the big hit. When you choke the club, it prevents you from cocking your wrists correctly and this defeats the whole purpose of the extra club length by shortening the swing arc. It also fouls up your lever system so you get less power out of your swing instead of more. With the light grip pressure and the longer driver, your wrists may cock a little later in your back-swing than you are used to. Don't fight it, just let your wrists set themselves in response to the momentum of your club-head as it swings back, around and up to the top of your swing.

You will find it useful to relax your neck and shoulders, making sure that your arms hang naturally from your shoulders as you bend from your hips to the ball. Natural arm hang will prevent you from reaching too far for the ball. While it may feel more powerful to reach for the ball by extending your arms away from the body, it is a sure way of losing your balance because your weight pulls you onto your toes as you swing to the top.

It is also a good idea to modify the height that you tee your ball. With the deep-faced driver the tendency is to tee the ball too low, so make sure that there is about a quarter of an inch of space between the top edge of your club and the bottom of the ball, just enough room to slip the thin shaft of a golf tee through. This will help you to catch the ball slightly on the up-swing so you can deliver maximum club-head mass to the ball at the moment of impact, thereby launching the ball at optimum trajectory.

Don't try to swing the club on a long arc because this will only lead to an over-swing. As we have already said, the squareness of contact is important to distance because off-center hits don't go as far, so don't try to hit it longer by swinging longer. Also, to make solid contact, swing within yourself and give your swing motion time to develop, starting back to the ball slowly, with gradually increasing momentum.

Basically, once you are properly fit, if you make the set-up adjustments above, the added length will get the job done. It is another case of "let" rather than "make."

Physical problems

M ost non-golfers do not consider golf to be a physically strenuous activity, and would not think that a golf swing could cause many injuries. But golfers know that although it may not cause the horrific damage associated with sports like football, boxing and car racing, there are many golf injuries that can limit or

Lee Trevino's career has been hampered by injuries that often afflict golfers as they age.

end your ability to play the game. There are physical problems too, such as hip degeneration or arthritis, that can be irritated by swinging a golf club and can significantly hamper your enjoyment of the game.

48

A golf swing looks effortless when demonstrated by an expert, but it is an athletic act that can channel four horsepower of energy and set the club-head moving at speeds up to 140 miles per hour, all in less than a second. A club-head moving at 100 miles per hour has an effective weight of 30 pounds, and to control it requires the active participation of almost every muscle in the body. So, while it may appear as though a golf swing does not involve physical exertion, a total body effort is actually required to generate the necessary power, transfer it to the club, and deliver it to the ball at impact.

This chapter outlines the most common physical problems among senior golfers, offering a way to compensate for injuries and, more importantly, avoid moves in a golf swing that can harm your body. However, it is important that you understand that this book is not intended to be a medical guide. If you are injured or ill, you should see your doctor. But the more you know about your golfing body, the easier it is to practice the best self-healing technique of all – prevention.

You weren't designed to swing a golf club

When you watch the twisting and odd-angled bending of a golf swing, it is no surprise that the part of the body most frequently injured by golfers is the back. The next most common injury is the mysterious "golfer's elbow," a problem that comes and goes seemingly at random, and can range from a nagging ache to a pain so debilitating that it is impossible to swing a club.

Shoulder injuries are also common, as are hand and wrist problems. Many injuries are caused by sudden over-use. For example, if you have not played golf for several months and then go on a golf vacation, it is unwise to hit 200 balls on the driving range on the first day. Accidental injuries also occur. Then there are the non-golf injuries too, many of which are a result of the aging process.

The American Physical Therapy Association says recreational golfers between the ages of 35 and 50 are more likely to be injured than any other age group. Why? First, many refuse to admit that they cannot play as they did when they were younger, and push themselves too hard. Second, those who live in colder climates do not exercise enough during the winter. When they emerge from hibernation, they place too much stress on unprepared muscles. Third, many do not take steps to avoid injuries. They are at the precarious stage of still having the strength to swing too hard, yet not being in condition to endure the strain. Seniors must realize that injury is likely to occur when they try to make their body perform like it did 25 years ago.

Shoulder problems

The shoulder is a complex structure that is comprised of four separate joints. The shoulder has three bones: the scapula, humerus, and clavicle. The joint is both versatile and vulnerable. In right-handed golfers, the most common injury is to the left shoulder because of the repetitive strain caused during the back-swing, especially at the top of the swing, and the pulling action of the down-swing as the left arm speeds back to the ball.

Rotator cuff

The rotator cuff muscles work to strengthen and stabilize the shoulder joint. The cuff is comprised of four muscles sharing a common tendon. Primarily, their function is to rotate the arm internally and externally. The rotator cuff is an important stabilizer of the shoulder for throwing-based athletes, such as baseball pitchers or football quarterbacks.

Quite simply, you know you have shoulder problems when you experience pain, especially when reaching up higher than your shoulder or making a sudden movement as in trying to catch something that's falling. Rotator problems also reveal themselves at night when they make it painful to sleep on the shoulder in question. Often an injured shoulder will also be tender when you press your finger at an angle under the shoulder joint at its outer edge. But the real tip off for the golfer is pain at the top of your swing, when the pressure is squarely on the cuff.

You may either have strained the tendon, the fibrous tissue that anchors the muscles to the bones of the shoulder girdle or, as is common in senior golfers, you may have actually have torn the muscle fibers. Recurring shoulder pain should definitely be referred to your doctor since it can also signal any number of potentially serious problems, from cancer, this is where it started for Paul Azinger, to heart disease. The latter can cause pain in the left shoulder on exertion, such as when climbing stairs.

Your doctor must make the diagnosis, and fortunately, if the problem is your rotator cuff, this need not mean the end of your golf career. By adopting the Senior Swing, you will place much less strain on your shoulder. At the top of the Senior Swing, the left arm is not at as acute an angle in relation to the shoulder as it is in a standard swing.

Remember that, although the shoulder has a larger range of motion than any other joint in the body, a golf swing places an incredible strain on it. Swinging an object above and behind the body while keeping the body bent is a very unusual and traumatic motion that pushes the highly functional shoulder joint to the maximum. Over time, it can literally wear out. By keeping your hands low and directly in front of your chest, the Senior Swing not only gives you the most direct route to the ball, but it also takes much of the strain off your shoulder, especially when combined with the moving coil technique described in Chapter 2.

Once your physician gives you the go-ahead to play golf you should do everything you can to avoid irritating the joint. In your first few weeks back, we recommend that you hit all your shots off a tee to be sure you don't jar your shoulder in its fragile state. You should definitely leave your long irons at home. The mis-hits common to long irons cause vibrations that make shoulders, elbows and hands throb with pain. It is easier to make solid contact with utility woods and you can hit them higher and softer than the long irons. Even with the modifications the Senior Swing offers, you will still be taxing the joint so, at any sign of pain, you should rest and ice your shoulder and call your doctor.

If you have pain but have confirmed that it is not due to a rotator cuff injury, it could be a strain where the tissue (most often muscle or a tendon) is simply stretched out of shape. With a strain there is soreness, but no evidence of joint instability, and the condition improves with rest. If you have torn the muscle or tendon – a more serious condition – rest may relieve the pain but it returns as soon as you start to play again.

The shorter back-swing of the Senior Swing can prevent irritation to the shoulder joint.

Elbow problems

Tendons are strong, fibrous tissues that connect muscle to bone. Tendonitis occurs when the tendon swells and becomes sore. There are several causes, the most common being overuse and/or overload of the muscles. Flexibility is important in preventing tendonitis – if you don't stretch properly you can cause problems of this kind. Working out too vigorously can also cause fibers in the tendon to tear.

Pain and a reduction in the range of motion are signs of tendonitis. The tendon can become so swollen that it actually makes a noise when it is used. Even though continued exercise may make the tendon feel better, do not keep going. Exercise can do much more harm than good in this situation. Rest is the first step on the road to recovery.

When you have "golfer's elbow" you will experience pain at the inside of your elbow.

Golfer's elbow is an inflammation of the tendons of the muscles that curl your arm, where they connect to the bones on the inside part of the elbow joint (with the palm up). Golfer's elbow usually affects the left elbow of right-handers and the right elbow of left-handers. Inflammation occurs because of repeated stress to the muscles that allow the forearm to flex. In golf, these muscles are placed under stress near the top of the backswing, as well as when the left arm straightens at impact (right-handers) and gives the left elbow a whip-like jolt.

The symptoms of golfer's elbow can either come on slowly or appear suddenly in various forms of severity – from a slight throb, to a pain so intense that it hurts to turn a door knob. There is pain on the inside, bony part of the elbow that juts out toward the body when you try to rotate the forearm inward or flex the wrist toward the body. Although it is called golfer's elbow, any athlete whose sport requires a sudden extension and rotation of the arm combined with a snap of the wrist is at risk. If left untreated, the elbow can deteriorate, develop bone chips, scar tissue, and even arthritis. Treatment includes resting the elbow and applying ice.

Once the symptoms subside, you should begin exercises to strengthen the forearm flexors. Start by simply flexing and extending the elbow through a full range of motion. Then do the forearm exercises described in Chapter 8 on fitness with very light weights.

Aside from these exercises, perhaps the best way to build up your forearms so they can cushion the shock to your elbow is to squeeze a soft rubber ball. It is an easy exercise to do and, in no time, your forearm muscles will be much stronger. Be sure to alternate hands frequently and also to roll the ball through your fingers, applying pressure as you go. Alternate between the last three fingers of each hand and the thumb and index finger, so you don't overdo one motion. Obviously, if you already have tendonitis, do not squeeze the ball – rest until the pain goes away.

The arm was not designed specifically to play golf, a sport where a solid object is struck at high speeds during an oblique rotation of the forearm. The forearm muscles that plug into your elbow are attached by a tendon that is really quite small considering all the work it does. For instance, to keep the club from twisting in the hand while the left forearm rotates through impact requires contraction of the forearm muscles. When the force of impact is transmitted to this undersized tendon, damage can occur, especially when you hit ball after ball. Overloading can so traumatize the tendon that, in its advanced stages, it is hard to turn a doorknob, to say nothing of hitting down on a 5-iron. The pain associated with golfer's elbow can ruin your game.

There are several things you can do to soothe this condition. The best remedy is to apply ice at the first sign of discomfort. The second is rest. The third is to improve your swing technique, using the Senior Swing, so you hit the ball more solidly and avoid the vibration associated with mis-hits. Also, while we do not endorse any products, it is a fact that many of today's tour professionals wear copper bracelets, and some use magnets. In one small study, Brazilian copper workers, who have their bodies exposed to copper as they work, were found to have a lower incidence of joint inflammation than the general population. That's not enough hard evidence, but if you don't mind an occasional green hue to your wrist, you might give a copper bracelet a try. By all reports, it is like chicken soup – it can't hurt.

The bent left arm

There has been a good deal of debate about whether to bend the left arm or keep it straight in the back-swing. We are of the opinion that you should keep your left arm straight. Usually the left arm bends because there is too little shoulder turn. This tends to lift the club to an overswing position which causes off-centered contact. In the Senior Swing, you do not need to bend your left arm if you use the moving coil, where your upper body moves laterally and you turn your left shoulder and chest behind the ball. Note, though, that we are advocating a straight left arm, not a stiff left arm locked in tension.

Elbow problems *continued*

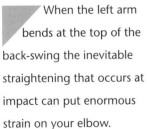 When the left arm bends at the top of the back-swing the inevitable straightening that occurs at impact can put enormous strain on your elbow.

The few modern experts who let their left arm bend do so only slightly. We believe that, when the left arm is allowed to bend excessively, an enormous level of force is exerted against the elbow joint as it straightens through impact. It is this force which can cause great amounts of irritation and injury to the joint.

The Senior Swing can also help reduce elbow problems, because the strong left hand grip allows you to hit the ball without an excessive forearm rotation, one of the most irritating and dangerous movements for a vulnerable elbow.

Hand problems

An injury to your only link to the club can put a quick end to your golf game. Other than an accident, the next most common source of golfing hand problems is arthritis. A slight mis-hit can cause a vibration that runs up the shaft and into the hands. This is an extremely painful experience for those with arthritic hands. In this case, a vicious circle often sets in. You know that impact may cause great pain, so you automatically pull away from the ball just before impact. This leads to contact on the toe of the club, and this off-center hit makes the vibrations even worse.

Arthritic hands can also prevent the golfer from closing fingers around the club. While it does not always help, you can try jumbo-sized grips that allow you to wrap your fingers more loosely around the club. You can also wear weight lifters' gloves that have open fingers and padding across the palms, which can dampen vibration. Another tactic is wearing an oversized glove on each hand and stuffing a thin sheet of foam rubber between glove and palm. We suggest you tee up every ball. Although this is against the rules of the game for any form of competition play, it will allow you to play a casual round with your friends. Also, remove the long irons and even medium length irons

If you have arthritis in your hands, jumbo grips and the padding in weight lifters' gloves may reduce the pain associated with gripping the club.

from your set of clubs. Club manufacturers not only offer the standard utility woods to replace long irons, but now have 7-, 9- and 11-woods that replace the mid-irons and make solid contact much easier. Club makers can also provide a number of vibration-decreasing devices that fit inside the club shaft and dampen the shock of impact.

Hip problems

If your right hip is injured, pivot on your left hip only.

The hip is a ball and socket joint that acts as a pivot center for the golf swing. The right hip serves as the pivot point in the back-swing (for right-handers) and the left hip is the pivot point during the down-swing and follow-through. This movement of pressure from the right hip to the left occurs without difficulty in a healthy younger golfer's swing. But if, as a senior, you have hip problems such as bursitis or arthritis, there are helpful adjustments you can make.

At address, narrow your stance and flare both feet a bit more than in the standard Senior Swing. Though it is not as efficient for power, you will put less stress on your hips the more you let your left foot rise in the back-swing. Be sure to relieve all pressure by making the proper finish, where your weight is on your left side and your right foot is balanced on its toe. This is the same strategy as the one you should use if you have a shoulder problem. Reduce coil (upper body turning against lower body) by turning your hips and your shoulders the same amount, and you will reduce the stress on your body.

The one-hip swing

Normally, the golf swing requires a body turn plus a weight shift that results in pivoting on both hips. But if one hip is out of commission golf-wise, you have to eliminate the weight shift but not the body turn. If your right hip is the problem, set up with the ball more forward in your stance and the majority of weight in your left hip. Keep your weight in your left hip throughout the entire swing. Although there is not a weight shift,

this allows you to make a sufficient body turn by rotating around your left hip and keeping pressure off your right hip.

If your left hip is the problem, do just the opposite – move the ball back and keep your weight in the right hip throughout the swing. It will take some practice, but you can hit the ball fairly well keeping your weight on just one hip.

For severe hip problems, you might try playing with a very narrow stance. This makes your swing much more upper body oriented and minimizes weight shift. But if you do, remember not to swing too hard.

If your left hip is injured, pivot on your right hip only.

Back problems

It is rare to find a good player, or for that matter any long-time golfer, who does not have some sort of back problem. This is because the nature of the game dictates that you swing at the ball while standing to the side of it. This introduces a twisting that strains the muscles and compresses the vertebrae in the lower back, an unusual angle that can lead to the malady know as "golfer's back." This is not to say that golf automatically ruins your back because, with the proper technique – in your case the Senior Swing – and attention to exercise and stretching, you can safely protect your back from the hazards of golf.

The Senior Swing is easier on the back than other variations of the golf swing. At the opposite end of the spectrum is the kind of swing that produces the "Reverse C" finish made famous by Jack Nicklaus and Johnny Miller in their prime. By far the most damaging, the "C" position results in high hands

If your back is injured, you can reduce potential for strain by letting your left heel rise and turning your lower body as much as your upper body.

at the top of the swing with the upper spine remaining stock still during the down-swing, both of which put enormous stress on the back. At impact, this configuration causes the arms and club to swing out from under the head, squeezing the discs in the lower back.

The errors more common to the amateur swing, such as bending and dipping the spine at impact, can also put strain on the muscles of the lower back. Muscle fatigue is common in this case and, if muscles are traumatized, spasms can occur. When they do, the muscles go into contraction, causing not only pain but possibly producing a damaging pull on the spinal cord.

Treatment for golfer's back ranges from the severe – surgery to repair herniated discs – to the less dramatic, such as moist heat, massage and, of course, rest. Instead of having to face any of these options, there are fortunately some preventive measures you can take to protect your back.

The first thing to do is to change your swing technique to the Senior Swing. With its floating coil, the S swing motion is more around your spine, which causes far less bending and stress on the back than the standard swing. Additionally, allowing the head to release at impact lets you stand up in the "I" finish in your follow-through, and this is a real back-saver.

If your back is really hurting, there are several adjustments you can make to the S swing:

◼ Move closer to the ball so you don't bend much from your hips. Stand almost upright with more knee flex to take pressure off your back. Narrow your stance and let your hips turn as much as they can, even if this involves raising your left heel so that, at the top of your swing, you are up on your left toe. Let your shoulders and hips turn about the same amount. This lessens coil but it also relieves the strain that the twist of coil puts on your back. Move the ball farther back and close your stance more than the normal S swing recommends, while strengthening both your right and left hand grip position by rotating your hands to the right. This will produce a lower, hooking, ball flight, and you will have to aim a little more to the right than normal, but at least your changes will allow you to keep playing.

◼ Keep fit in general and do special lower back exercises in particular. See Chapter 8 on fitness.

◼ Be careful of your back and avoid heavy lifting. When you bend over, even to do something as benign as brushing your teeth, keep your knees flexed and your back straight rather than hunching. Lifting a suitcase or your clubs from the trunk of your car is a real back-breaker.

◼ Take precautions on the course. When you are teeing a ball or picking it out of the hole, flex your knees and squat rather than doing any stiff-legged bending. Better still, there is a suction cup device you can buy that fits on the grip end of your putter that will save your back from having to pick the ball up out of the hole.

Bifocals

You should not wear bifocals when you play golf, so use only single-vision "distance" glasses. In order to view the ball through the top "distance" part of the bifocal lenses, you will have to tuck your head down at address. If you do, you will restrict your ability to turn and be forced to lift the club in your back-swing. This ruins your posture and dramatically reduces your own ability to produce the coil necessary for power.

Chapter four

Putting and chipping

T he short game can be a great equal-izer, giving every level of player the chance to shave strokes from their score. A good short game does not require peak physical condition or superb coordina-tion; it only requires the application of a few solid fundamentals combined with a win-ning strategy.

The winning strategy for a great short game is simple: play the percentages. By this, we mean play the shot with the least margin for error and the greatest opportunity for suc-cess. To do so, use the following guidelines. Ideally, always putt the ball when you can, even if it is off the green. If you can't putt, choose the shot that is most similar to a putt, the low, running chip shot. If you need a slightly higher shot, take your sand-wedge and hit a low trajectory pitch. Your next choice is the standard pitch, with the high trajectory pitch serving as your last resort.

Arnold Palmer, golf's legendary King.

Putting fundamentals

A good putt, like every other shot in golf, is a blend of correct distance and direction. To produce both, the basic putting fundamen-tals require you to do four things:

■ make contact with the ball in the center of the club-face,

■ have the putter head moving level to the ground at the correct speed,

■ have the putter moving along the line you want the ball to start on,

■ have the club-face facing this line at the moment of impact.

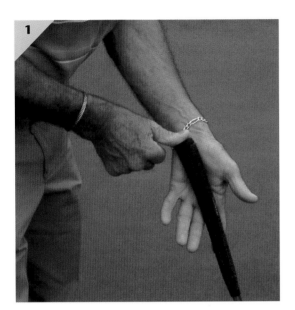

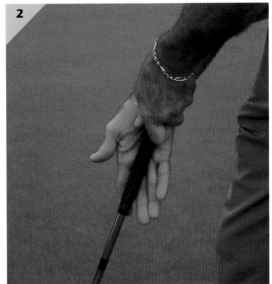

The stroke motion grip

You will use this grip for both putting and chipping, since it encourages accuracy. Grip the club in your palms rather than your fingers. Even though your hands are separated, your palms face each other so that your hands work as a unit. This also means that your right palm should face the target, which naturally helps direct the putter head down the target line. Your thumbs should be on top of the grip to prevent your hands from twisting during your stroke.

Alignment

The primary alignments in putting are of the club-face, your eyes and your shoulders. Where the club-face points at impact determines the starting direction of the ball. The direction your shoulders point in determines the path of your swing. And since the tendency is to putt where you look, your eye alignment

also affects the path of your stroke. To make sure these alignments are in the correct relationship to one another to produce an effective shot, use the following procedure:

Club-face alignment

First, set your putter square to the line you want the ball to start on, directly behind the ball. For a straight putt this would be the straight line from the ball to the hole. But since most putts curve or break according to the slopes of the green, you will need to set the putter square to the line you want the ball to start on.

Shoulder alignment

The next step is to align your shoulders square (parallel) to your starting line. A closed position at address causes an inside-to-out path; an open position produces an outside-to-in path. Either mistake in your stance will cause the ball to roll off your intended line.

1 Left hand grip: place the grip in the palm of your hand.

2 Right hand grip: right palm faces target and grip is in the palm of the hand.

3 Completed grip: the back of the left hand faces the target and the thumbs are on top of the shaft.

Putting fundamentals *continued*

Shoulder alignment: the shoulders are parallel to the target line.

Eye alignment: when the eyes are over the ball the arms hang comfortably from the shoulders.

Eye alignment

Third, bend forward from your hip sockets and position your eyes over the ball or slightly inside the line you want the ball to start out on. As we have said, your putting stroke follows your eyes, and this set-up configuration allows you to see the correct line to the hole and square your shoulders to that line.

Hand position

By bending from the hips your hands should fall directly below your shoulders. This puts your arms and hands in position for a straight-back-and-through stroke. If the hands are positioned inside the shoulders, the path tends to travel on an outside-square-outside arc. If the hands are outside the shoulder line, the club-head travels on a path inside-square-inside. In either case, an inconsistent contact is the likely result.

Ball position

Play the ball just slightly forward of the center of your stance. You will know you have the position correct when the shaft of the putter points at the mid-line of your body with the putter face centered behind the ball. To preserve the loft of the putter make sure the shaft is vertical rather than tilted toward or away from the target.

The putting stroke

The stroke we recommend is a pendulum motion, very similar to the swing of a pendulum in a grandfather clock, where the back and forth movement is of equal length in both directions. All pendulums swing from a pivot and, in putting, your pivot point is the top of your spine. This point must remain stationary, as your shoulders and arms swing the putter back and forth in a rocking motion. Maintain a constant distance between your elbows throughout the stoke – neither narrowing nor widening the gap between them – to ensure a constant bottom to the putter's arc. Your hands are only required to hold the putter steady and straight; it is the rocking of your shoulders that controls the length of the stroke.

The long putter

If your hands have developed a mind of their own when it comes to putting, the long putter may be the answer. With this type of club, your left hand anchors the putter against your sternum and your right hand has the job it has been fighting for: control of the stroke.

Set up to the long putter by bending forward slightly from your hips. This puts your eyes slightly inside the target line. Position the ball slightly forward of the center of your stance, with the shaft of the club vertical. With your left palm facing your body, place your left thumb on top of the handle to secure the top of the shaft against your sternum. Your left elbow should point at the target. With your right palm facing the target, hold the club across your palm, midway down the shaft. The stroke itself is a pure pendulum action with the top of the putter remaining fixed throughout the stroke and your right hand controlling the motion. It takes about two weeks to get a feel for the long putter.

The long putter causes less back strain and returns control to your hands.

Putting strategy

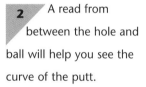

1 First read the putt from behind the hole.

2 A read from between the hole and ball will help you see the curve of the putt.

3 Finally, read the putt from behind the ball to determine your line.

To determine the line of your putt, first walk behind the hole and look back down the line to the ball. As you do this, take careful note of the slope around the hole because, since the ball will roll most slowly in this area, it is most affected by whatever slope that may exist. Once you have established the dominant break, go to the lower side of the slope, half way between the ball and the hole. From the low side you can determine the severity of the slope. Your final read takes place from behind the ball. Here, confirm your findings from the other areas and determine the line you want to start the ball rolling along.

Following a routine

To gain consistency in your putting, you must have a set pre-shot routine in which you automatically perform the same actions in the same timespan. In pressure situations, this allows you to putt as you would at any other time.

After you have read the details of the putt, approach the ball perpendicular to your chosen line. Standing slightly back from the ball, look at the hole and make a practice stroke to feel the distance and line of the putt. Then look at the ball and simulate the stroke you want to make. Slide the putter forward so the sweet spot on the head is directly behind the ball. Step forward and set your feet square to the line you want the ball to start on. Finally, check that the putter head, shoulders and eyes

To prepare your muscles for the distance of the putt always take your practice strokes looking at the target. This gives your brain the information necessary to produce the appropriate energy to hit the ball the right distance. On uphill putts, stand farther away from the hole than your ball actually is to program a firmer stroke; on downhill putts, stand closer to the hole to program an easier stroke.

are aligned correctly, as described earlier.

Once you are in position over the ball, you should have a rhythm that never varies. Learn this by counting to yourself as follows: look down the line to the hole in one count, bring your eyes back to the ball on the second count, swing the putter back on three and through on the count of four. If you prefer two looks at the hole, add the additional counts. If you need to look back more than twice, you are clearly unsure of the line. Step away and re-evaluate. Once you ingrain a routine and rhythm, the great benefit is that your stroke becomes automatic, especially under pressure. Your goal is to eliminate thoughts of putting mechanics as you flow through a routine that begins by carefully reading the line and distance and is dedicated to making a confident stroke based on that.

To die or dunk

For short putts, the "never up, never in" motto applies. For any putt you feel you can hole, you should have an aggressive policy. Make sure the you stroke the ball firmly enough to dunk into the back of the hole. An added benefit of being firm with short putts is that the firm roll makes the ball less susceptible to the spike marks and footprints that inevitably collect around the cup.

If you are good at judging distances, you should also be aggressive with medium length putts. As a good putter, you will be able to handle the three-footer coming back if you miss the first putt. If your distance skills are poor, plan on hitting a "dying" putt, where the ball only trickles into the hole. If you miss, you will only have a tap-in remaining.

1 Take a practice stroke while looking at the hole to get a feel for distance.

2 Next, aim the face square to the target line.

3 Then set your body square and look back down the line to confirm your target.

Putting strategy *continued*

Regardless of your game plan, try to make sure that, if you miss the initial putt, your next putt is manageable for your skill level.

Putts longer than 15 feet should be played as "dying" putts, as should medium length putts on very fast or severely undulating greens. With long putts, the challenge is to avoid three-putting. The odds against holing a putt greater than 15 feet are high, so, in keeping with the strategy of playing the percentages, plan on "dying" the ball around the hole from outside 15 feet.

Studies show that, around the green, accuracy is greatest when you roll a ball to the hole rather than fly it there. This obviously means you are most accurate when putting the ball. But when you are just off the green and can't putt, a low running chip produces almost as much accuracy as putting. For maximum chipping accuracy, we recommend a chipping technique that is almost identical to your putting stroke.

1 Move your hands down the iron until it matches the length of your putter.

2 Your weight will settle naturally on your left foot.

3 The club's decending angle will propel the ball into the air.

Chipping

The concept

The key concept is to make chipping an extension of your putting stroke. The chip shot is used when you are less than six yards from the green where conditions allow for a very low, short ball flight and a lot of roll.

To make chipping as similar to putting as possible, use your putting grip and the same pendulum motion. But, since the ball needs to fly a short distance, there are some differences. You will use an iron, but adapt it by raising it on its toe to make the shaft upright like a putter, which allows for the straight-back-and-through stroke characteristic of the pendulum motion. Grip down on the iron until it matches the length of your putter and use a pendulum style, shoulder-controlled motion, with minimal lower body movement and no wrist action.

Since chipping requires a stable lower body, your stance width should be narrow. The short motion does not allow time for a weight transfer, and the power one might produce is counter-productive in any case. To anchor your lower body and encourage your weight to stay on your left side throughout the stroke, open your stance by dropping your left foot back from the target line. Your weight will settle naturally to your left.

Position the ball off the inside of your right foot, and angle the shaft toward the target so your hands are opposite your left thigh. This produces a descending angle of attack that propels the ball into the air. Since your shoulders control the path of your stroke, be sure they are square to your target line. Your wrists should remain inactive throughout the stroke.

4 Make sure your shoulders are square to the target line.

Set the club on its toe for a chip shot.

Choosing the correct club

Many golfers automatically reach for a favorite club when chipping, such as a 7-iron, regardless of the situation. Instead of making one club fit all situations, we recommend you use the iron with the correct loft for each situation, a range of clubs from 3-iron to sand-wedge all adjusted according to the chipping fundamentals outlined above. This way, instead of varying your technique with one club, you can fit the club to the shot and keep your technique consistent, just as you do with your full swing.

The key to consistent chipping can be summarized as follows: use one stroke for all situations, and let your different clubs produce the different distances and different amounts of flight and roll you need. The longer the rolling portion of the chip shot, the less lofted the club. The shorter the roll, the more lofted the club.

Flight-to-roll ratio

Depending on the loft of the club, there is a ratio between the amount of flight and roll for a correctly played chip in this style. This is the basis for correct club selection.

Club	Flight	Roll
Sand-wedge	1 part	1 part
Pitching-wedge	1 part	2 parts
9-iron	1 part	3 parts
8-iron	1 part	4 parts
7-iron	1 part	5 parts
6-iron	1 part	6 parts
5-iron	1 part	7 parts
4-iron	1 part	8 parts
3-iron	1 part	9 parts

Notice that the lofted clubs, such as your 9-iron and wedges, have a more even balance between flight and roll distance. Thus a chip with your sand-wedge (set up and played as described above) flies as far in the air as it rolls on the ground. The lofted clubs should

therefore be used when the hole is cut close to the edge of the green, a situation where there is little room for roll.

As the space between the edge of the green and the hole increases, you need more roll, so your club selection moves from the short irons, through the mid-irons and finally to the long irons, where the ball has minimal flight time and maximum roll. Since every chip shot requires some flight time to land on the green, your 1-and 2-iron are not an option. They do not have enough loft, once adjusted for chipping. When you need an extra long chip shot, use your 3-iron and stroke it more firmly.

The two constants

Keep in mind two constants for every chip, the landing area and the number 12. The landing area should always be one yard onto the green whenever possible. This allows the ball maximum roll distance, which is best for

68

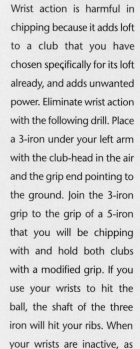

Wrist action is harmful in chipping because it adds loft to a club that you have chosen specifically for its loft already, and adds unwanted power. Eliminate wrist action with the following drill. Place a 3-iron under your left arm with the club-head in the air and the grip end pointing to the ground. Join the 3-iron grip to the grip of a 5-iron that you will be chipping with and hold both clubs with a modified grip. If you use your wrists to hit the ball, the shaft of the three iron will hit your ribs. When your wrists are inactive, as they should be, you will feel the pressure of the shaft against your left arm.

accuracy, while giving you an easy target to aim at and enough margin for error in case of a slight mis-hit.

Use the chart to understand the second constant, the number 12. Take, for example, a chip that requires one part flight and five parts roll. The chart indicates the need for a 7-iron. Add the roll (five) to the club (seven) and the sum is the constant 12. It is the same for all the clubs in the chart. Thus, the constant of 12 is the total of the club and roll added together.

The two variables

In addition to the two constants, there are two variables associated with every chip which you should measure: the distance the ball should fly and the distance it should roll. To determine the first, simply count the number of steps from your ball to the constant landing area – one yard onto the green. The number of steps determines the distance the ball should fly.

To determine the second variable, the amount of roll, count the number of paces from the landing area (not from the ball) to

Wrist action is harmful while chipping because it adds power and loft that you do not want *(above left)*. For chipping correctly keep your wrists inactive *(above right)*.

Choosing the correct club
continued

the hole. With both variables on hand, you are now ready to figure the flight-to-roll ratio. For example, if you have 5 paces from the ball to the landing area, and 15 additional paces from the landing area to the hole, the ball will have a flight-to-roll ratio of 5 to 15, equivalent to 1 part flight to 3 parts roll.

Having determined the flight-to-roll ratio, the final step is to subtract the roll part – 3 in this example – from the constant 12, to determine your chipping club. In this example, 3 from 12 is 9, therefore the club for this situation is a 9-iron because it produces 1 part flight and 3 parts roll.

You may face a situation where the flight-to-roll ratio is not easily simplified. For example, you may have 3 steps from the ball to landing area, and 16 steps from the landing area to the hole. In this case, just adjust your ratio to 3 to 15 and simplify it to 1 part flight and 5 parts roll. Subtract the 5 from the constant of 12, and a 7-iron is the right club for this situation.

Adjust the club selection depending on the slope of the green. When chipping uphill, for example, adjust for the slope by choosing a 5-iron instead of a 6-iron. If you are chipping downhill, change from a 6-iron to a 7-iron.

Once you practice calculating the flight-to-roll ratio, you will begin to see every chip as having a certain amount of flight compared to the amount of roll. Soon you will be able to do the calculations subconsciously

and just reach for the correct club. Note that since the flight distance is always reduced to one part, you simply need to evaluate how many times greater the amount of distance the ball has to roll is than the amount it has

A common error made while chipping is trying to help the ball into the air. To do so, golfers usually fall back on their right sides on their through swing to try to get under the ball. This leads to one of two disasters: a fat shot that finishes well short of the hole, or a thin shot that scurries over to the far side of the green.

To prevent this, practice some chips by placing a board perpendicular to the target line about a foot behind the ball. If your weight is on your right side during the back-swing or through swing, the club-head will hit the board *(see the left-hand photo)*. When your weight stays left, the club-head never touches the board *(see the right-hand photo)*.

to fly. For example, let's say that you judge your ball as being about 4 yards from the landing area (1 part roll) and then figure that it is six times that distance from the landing area to the hole. Subtract that 6 from the constant of 12, and the correct club is a 6-iron. After you master this short cut, you will move to the next level: you will find that you say to yourself, "It looks like a 5-iron chip," and you will be correct.

Chapter five

Pitching and bunker play

Senior PGA Tour player Mike Hill hits a short pitch shot to the green.

P itching and bunker play require a swing motion rather than the stroke motion employed in putting and chipping. For this reason, you should use your full swing grip for pitching and sand shots, and adapt your other pre-swing fundamentals from the standards established in Chapter 1 on the set-up.

Pitch shots fly higher and roll less than chip shots, allowing you to fly the ball over obstacles, such as a bunker or heavy rough, and have it land softly on the green. But pitch shots have a greater margin for error, so

The pitching technique

are your last choice in the short game strategy of playing the percentages.

Golfers often have difficulty with pitching because they make unusual adjustments to their set-up and swing. Your pitching game will improve if you remember that a pitch shot is nothing more than a miniature version of your full swing. Keep in mind the four essentials of pitching and you will avoid the mistakes that commonly occur:

▣ The club-face aims at the target. This may sound simplistic, but the first thing you should do is aim your club-face directly at the target. Once that is done, adjust your shoulders to the type of shot you want to hit. Closed shoulders (pointing to the right of target), with the ball back of the center of your stance, produce a lower, running pitch; open shoulders (pointing to the left of target), with the ball off your left heel, produce a higher than normal pitch shot.

▣ The shaft of the club should point at the center of your body. At address, the grip end of the shaft should point to the center line of your body. If the shaft leans ahead of the center of your body, the bounce and loft of the club is reduced, making it difficult for the club to slide under the ball. When you adjust the ball position to change the trajectory of the shot, the shaft must still point at the center of your body.

▣ The swing is of equal distance back and through. How far you swing the club back determines how far you swing the club through. Your back-swing and through swing should be mirror images of each other. A symmetrical back-swing

On a perfect lie, the club-head is soled flush to the ground. For tighter lies, rest the club-head more on the toe, stand closer to the ball and position the ball more toward the toe of the club. This reduces bounce and wrist cock, which helps prevent a mis-hit shot. When the ball is buried in the grass, set the club-head more on its heel and stand farther from the ball, but keep the ball in the center of the club-face – you don't want to bring the hosel into play. This increases the bounce of the club without adding loft and expands the potential hitting surface. This simple adjustment also lowers your hands, presetting your wrists to create a steeper angle of attack.

Be sure to aim the club-face at the target

The grip end of the club points at the center of your body.

73

The pitching technique *continued*

Swing is of equal length on both sides of the ball.

The arms swing along the shoulder line.

and through swing occur naturally unless you try to add or subtract force in your down-swing. A short back-swing and a long through swing usually combine to produce a thin shot that flies lower and farther than expected. A long back-swing and a short follow-through usually produce a fat shot where contact occurs behind the ball.

■ Your arms swing along your shoulder line. The last pitching essential is that the club should always swing along the shoulder line. When your shoulders are open, the club should swing out-to-in, relative to the target line. When the shoulders are square, the club should swing along the target line, an inside-square-inside swing path. When the shoulders are closed the club should swing on an inside-to-out path. Thus, the path of the club-head always follows the path of the shoulders. This eliminates the need to try consciously to lift the ball, cut across it, or hit down on it. Simply let the club swing on the path established by your shoulders.

If you utilize these essentials in pitching, the shot becomes as simple as setting up correctly and letting your club swing free of manipulation and compensation.

Controlling the distance

You control the distance of your pitch shots by the way you arrange your body at address and the length you swing the club. The shorter pitch shots are played from a narrow stance where your weight starts, stays and finishes on your left side. To set up for the short pitch, open your stance by dropping your left foot back from the target line. Don't overdo the openness by trying to copy the pros on TV. Remember that your full swing stance is a bit closed, so you will only open your stance slightly. By opening your stance, you automatically reduce your ability to turn, which consequently restricts the

The key to distance control is keeping your body rotating through the ball.

You want to land pitch shots on the green, rather than short of it, because the surface is the most perfectly manicured on the golf course and, therefore, offers a consistency that is easy to judge. Give yourself plenty of room for error by planning to land the ball at least a yard onto the green. If you have a lot of green to work with because the pin is in the middle or back, hit a low trajectory pitch. If the pin is tucked in, with not much landing area between the edge of the green and the hole, hit a high trajectory pitch that will land softly and stop quickly.

The pitching technique *continued*

length of your back-swing. In addition, an open stance effectively shortens your left leg, which causes more weight to settle on your left side. As the distance of the pitch increases, progressively lessen the amount you adjust your set-up until you arrive back at your full swing set-up for a short iron.

Grip lower on the club for shorter shots and higher on the club for longer shots. By gripping down you shorten the effective length of the club, which reduces the width of your swing arc and results in reduced distance.

The final distance factor is, the shorter the shot, the shorter the swing; the longer the shot, the longer the swing. Make sure not to add any extra power to your down-swing – that is not a reliable way to produce the correct distance. If you swing the club past the ball the same amount as you swing it away from the ball, you don't have to add or subtract any power. Use the concept of a pendulum, where the club swings equally back and through, and you will consistently produce accurate distances with solid contact.

Trajectory

The trajectory, or height of your shot, is controlled by two factors: ball position and the movement of the right arm. The farther

For higher trajectory pitch shots, move the ball forward in your stance.

For lower trajectory pitch shots, move the ball back in your stance.

forward (toward the left foot) you position the ball in your stance, the higher and softer the shot. The farther back in your stance you position the ball, the lower and more rolling the shot. Therefore, to hit a high, soft shot, position the ball forward in your stance. In normal pitch shots, the ball is located in the center of the stance, and to produce low, running shots, move the ball back in your stance.

One note of caution: as the ball moves forward in your stance, your shoulders will open; as it moves back in your stance, your shoulders close. When you change the ball position to vary the trajectory of your pitch shots, let the club swing on your shoulder line.

The right arm

For the high soft shot, the right arm should bend immediately during the take-away to open the club-face and elevate the club-head. Then, in the down-swing, the right elbow should stay close to the right side as the left arm extends with the knuckles of the left hand facing the sky.

To hit the low running pitch, your right arm bends very late in the back-swing for longer pitches and not at all for very short pitch shots. This hoods and closes the club-face for minimum loft and maximum roll. If you keep your right arm straight in the down-swing, the left arm should fold automatically.

1 Swing length controls distance – use a short swing for a short pitch.

2 Medium swing produces a medium pitch.

3 Using a fuller swing will yield a full pitch.

Bunker play

Green-side bunker play

Rule one when you find yourself stuck in the bunker is get out on your first attempt! To do so, there are two types of bunker shot that every golfer must learn to play effectively.

The first one is played from a good lie. The second technique is used from a bad lie, where part or all of the ball is actually buried in the sand. When the lie is good, you play a splash shot; when the ball is buried however, you play an explosion shot.

Raymond Floyd has had a spectacular professional career, in part because of a superb short game.

The splash shot

The splash shot requires displacement of the sand beneath the ball, which, in turn, lifts the ball into the air. The majority of our students misunderstand the fundamental of hitting the sand rather than the ball.

Splash shot set-up

The first thing you must do to understand the complete concept of the splash shot is to learn the proper set-up for distance control and accuracy. Step one requires that you open the club-face. The shorter the shot, the more the club-face needs to be opened and it is vital that you open the face before you take your grip. If you grip the club with a square face and roll your arms to open it, your arms will naturally return the face square at impact. Since your goal is to hit the sand behind the ball, don't grip down on the club. To preserve the loft of the club be sure the shaft points at the center-line of the body. Leaning the shaft ahead of the ball decreases the loft.

Step two requires that you rotate your stance open until the opened club-face aims at the target. Anchor your weight on your left side, where it should stay throughout the shot. Position the ball forward in your stance. This opens your shoulders and allows you to swing the club down your shoulder line on an out-to-in swing path that slices the ball out of the sand.

There are two other key points of set-up for the splash shot: dig your feet into the sand, and stand farther from the ball. By digging your feet in, you gain stability and ensure that the club-head contacts the sand before the ball. When you grip the club at its full length and dig your feet in, the club automatically bottoms out at the same level as your feet, hitting into the sand behind the ball instead of at the ball. Since digging in

Feeling
the bounce

Bury a painted 2-inch by 4-inch board vertically in the sand along your target line, so that the four inch side of the board is flush with the sand. Address the middle of the board and swing, allowing the bounce on the bottom of the club-head to skim the board without striking it.

Now place a pile of sand on the board. Use the same skimming motion and the sand will fly onto the green. Next, place a ball on top of the pile of sand. Ignore the ball and repeat the same motion. Both the ball and the sand will fly onto the green. Once you have a feel for the club-head skimming rather than digging into the sand, you will have the trick of the splash shot, and be able to hit the ball cleanly out of the sand with ease.

For a splash shot, open the club-face before you grip the club.

79

The splash shot *continued*

your feet moves the hosel of the club closer to the ball, you must stand farther from the ball by the same amount that you dig your feet in.

The final set-up key involves the position of your head – simply keep it in the middle of your shoulders rather than tilting it right or left.

The swing itself is mostly a shoulder and arm motion, where your weight stays on your left side throughout the shot. Your lower body does not stay rigid, however. Instead it should be allowed to respond to the movement of your upper body. As with pitching, be sure to swing the club along your shoulder line. The pace of your swing should match the distance you need to hit the ball: Slow pace, short shot; faster pace, longer shot.

Splash shots displace the sand beneath the ball, lifting the ball upwards.

Splash shot summary

■ Position the ball forward in your stance.

■ Open the club-face and then take your grip.

■ Open your stance until the club-face aims at the target.

■ Dig your feet into the sand for stability and stand further from the ball by the same amount you dig your feet in.

■ Point the butt end of the club at the center line of your body.

■ To hit the ball a shorter distance, open your stance and club-face more. Set up with more weight on your left side and swing the club at a slower pace.

■ To hit the ball farther, set up less openly with a squarer club-face, a wider stance, and swing the club at a faster pace.

■ Make sure your weight starts, stays, and finishes on your left side.

Buried bunker shot

Hitting the ball from a buried lie is quite different from playing a ball that is sitting up on the sand. Since the ball is buried, you need to take a deeper cut of the sand with your sand-wedge. To accomplish this, move the ball back in your stance and close the club-face. With the leading edge exposed and the bounce minimized, the sand-wedge digs into the sand rather than splashing through it.

Using a combination of hands and arms, swing the club directly up and down to create a descending blow into the sand that surrounds the back of the ball. This descending angle, along with the closed club-face, causes the club to dig deeply into the sand and pop the ball out. Because the club digs, the sand stops the momentum of the club and there is little or no follow-through. Too often, golfers try to help the ball up out of this type of lie. Unfortunately, this may propel the ball deeper into the sand or result in thin contact that sends the ball on a flat trajectory – straight under the lip of the bunker.

A steep "up and down" swing is required for the buried bunker shot.

1 For the buried bunker shot move the ball back in your stance and close the club face.

2 Swing the club directly up and down.

3 Bring the club down at a descending angle and dig it deeply into the sand.

4 The sand will slow the club and there will be little follow-through.

Buried bunker shot *continued*

When the correct technique is employed, expect the ball to fly on a lower trajectory and run farther. Even the pros have trouble controlling the distance of this shot, so your goal is simply to get the ball on the green.

Explosion shot summary

■ Close the club-face slightly before taking your grip.

■ Position the ball back in your stance.

■ Using only your arms and hands, strike a descending blow just behind the ball. The club-head will bury in the sand so don't try for a normal follow-through.

■ Allow for very little back-spin, a much lower trajectory and a lot of roll.

■ Don't try to hit a spectacular shot – take your medicine and just get the ball on the green.

Fairway bunkers

Fairway bunker shots are hard for average players because they try to get too much out of the shot. The fairway bunker is aptly named a hazard and therefore requires a special technique, combined with good course management.

Club selection

Before making your club selection, first check the lie of the ball, second the height of the bunker's lip, and only then the distance to your target. The lie of the ball determines the type of shot you can play. The lip determines what club you will need to produce the necessary trajectory to get out of the bunker. Once these conditions are satisfied, your last consideration is the length you want to hit the shot.

If you have a poor lie, where the ball is sitting down into the sand, your only choice is to take your sand-wedge and hit the ball back to the fairway. If you have a good lie, where

the ball sits up on top of the sand, next check the lip of the bunker. Regardless of the distance you "want" the ball to travel, you need a club with ample loft to clear the lip safely. You can only consider the length of the shot if the lie and the lip conditions are favorable. You won't hit the ball as far from a fairway bunker as you do from grass, so take at least one more club, if the lip allows you to. But if the distance calls for a 5-iron and the lip requires the trajectory of a 7-iron, you will have to go with the 7-iron.

The set-up

Your goal from a fairway bunker is to pick the

▶ Play the ball in the middle of your stance. Wedge your right foot against the sand and dig your left foot into the sand slightly.

ball cleanly off the sand. The following elements of your set-up are dedicated to achieving this goal: Play the ball in the middle of your stance to catch it before the club bottoms out. Grip down on the club about an inch, which shortens the shaft and also allows you to make a more controlled swing.

For stability, widen and open your stance, anchoring the majority of your weight on your left leg. Wedge your right foot against the sand with your right knee angled in toward the target. Be sure your shoulders are square, even though your feet and hips are open.

Catching the ball first

Your goal is to pick the ball off the sand so it is much better to hit the ball slightly thin rather than too fat. Your set-up guards against the dreaded fat shot, but it is important to think "thin to win." If you do catch

the ball slightly thin, it may not look pretty but the result is usually good. A fat shot would leave the ball in the bunker.

Once you have the concept – thin to win – make a three-quarter swing leaving most of your weight in your left hip throughout. Your hips turn in sympathy with your upper body motion, but you should not make a weight transfer. By reducing weight transfer, you decrease the possibility of slipping or sinking into the sand at the top of your swing – a sure way to hit the sand before you contact the ball.

Our last piece of advice is to make getting the ball back in play your priority. For this reason you should never use more than a 5-iron from a fairway bunker. Long irons have too little loft and fairway woods have too long a shaft. Both choices create too many possibilities for error, so stick with your middle to short irons from the fairway bunker.

The fairway bunker shot requires that you hit the ball before the sand.

Star swings

Chapter Six

84

In this chapter, you will see fine examples of Senior PGA Tour Players who have successfully maintained their golf skills while adapting their swings and their games to their changing bodies. As we stated in our first book, *Play Better Golf*, in 1995, "good golf swings, in order to satisfy the laws of physics (which they all must do), evolve based on body type, personality, the demands of the environment, and often, though not always, under the watchful eye of a masterful teacher. Thus swing elements are assembled based on the individual differences of the player."

The same is true for you as a senior – with one added element. Not only is your swing a product of the factors stated above, you must also adapt it based on the effects the aging process has on your body. In Chapter Two, we offer a detailed plan for you to do just that. In this chapter, as you look to these successful senior golfers for a role model, remember that they too have gone through a similar process. But since they all have played golf continuously for most of their lives, the process has been gradual and may have gone unnoticed by both player and casual observer alike, but you can be sure changes have occurred.

However, copying an elite player's swing can be dangerous, especially for seniors. So as you study the swings of these players, remem-

ber that, for the most part, they've stayed in shape, they play most every day, hit a lot of practice balls and their mechanics are still superb. So, you may not see all of the swing features we recommend to you – like a strong grip, wide stance or a back ball position – because they don't need them. But if you think your swing has deteriorated because of aging, you probably do need them to enjoy your game in the future as you have in the past.

The point is, we did not design the Senior Swing for Tour players, we designed it for the senior amateur. Since tour players play golf for a living, and have done so most of their lives, they are more flexible and, of course, more skilled. For some of them, the modifications we recommend to you would be too extreme a change from the basic and successful swing they developed long ago. Therefore, you won't see all of them using as wide or as closed a stance; you may not see the strong left handgrip that many senior amateurs need – not yet anyway.

So while you should view these star swings with this warning in mind, there is still much to be learned from their time-tested techniques. Though their set-up positions and swings may vary, there are fundamental elements all of these players have in common. The key is to understand how they all have personalized their swings to produce solid, powerful contact. Our goal is to help you see their similarities, in light of their differences, which is exactly why they have been included in this book.

Senior PGA Tour star Jim Albus at the PGA Championship at the PGA National Resort.

Dave Stockton

In 1964, Dave Stockton joined the PGA Tour. He had 11 career victories, including two PGA Championships, in '70 and '76. He joined the Senior Tour in '91 and in six years he has had 13 victories, including the US Senior Open in '96. He has won at least twice in each of his last four seasons, narrowly missing the title in '95. A two-time Ryder Cup Team member, he captained the '91 US Team. An all-around talent, Stockton is famed for his short game wizardry.

Ball Position

This face-on view shows you proper ball position. Here Stockton is hitting a 6-iron so the ball is correctly positioned in the middle of his stance. But remember that ball position varies with the club you are using. For medium to short irons, position the ball in the center of your stance. For long irons and utility woods position the ball one ball-width forward of the center of your stance; one ball width further forward for the driver.

Dave Stockton's is not a power-house swing, nor is it picture perfect, but it produces championship level golf that has endured for decades. Stockton is mentally tough; he plays for money and, is not locked up in swing mechanics. He is a tenacious competitor who can manipulate the flight of the ball to position himself in scoring range.

1 Stockton has a big chest and moderate flexibility, features he accommodates with adjustments to his set-up. His spine is inclined, not curved, so there's no hunch in his back. By bending from his hip joints, Stockton has prepared them to serve as centers of rotation, assuring a full and unrestricted hip turn during his swing. These set-up features are ideal for most senior amateurs with large chests and reduced flexibility. By flexing his knees just slightly, his lower leg is vertical, thereby distributing his weight over the balls of his feet. Stockton keeps his chin up and, therefore, has ample room to turn his left shoulder behind the ball. If you tuck your chin down onto your chest, you run the risk of blocking your shoulder turn and this limits your power.

2 A take-away does not last long, but how you start your swing often determines how it ends. Stockton's hands, arms, chest and the club move away from the ball in unison. His hands move along the line of his toes and, because he is playing from a slightly closed position, the club-head moves gently inside the target line to help ensure that his swing path will be inside-to-out through impact.

3 As the take-away ends, Stockton's weight moves onto his right hip which is the axis that his lower body turns around in the back-swing. There is absolutely no independent lifting of the arms – it is the folding of his right arm that elevates the club-head and the momentum of his back-swing that will further cock his wrists.

4 At the top of his swing his wrists are completely cocked and, even though his hands are not high, the club-head is well above him. Cocking the wrists not only provides the necessary swing arc but also the power of leverage, generated by the 90 degree angle formed by his left arm and the club-shaft. His short, tight swing is completely under control at the top.

5 Here you can see the literal definition of "the down-swing." Stockton's hands and arms drop straight down before the club-head moves out toward the target line. This puts him in perfect position to turn through the ball and square the club-face. His right shoulder is in an ideal position with no hint of over-the-top movement.

6 In photo 5, just before impact, Dave's right arm was still folded and both feet were firmly planted on the ground. Here with his left hip serving as his pivot-point, he releases the club-head to the ball by straightening his right arm. This causes the toe of the club to rotate over the heel through impact, another move which squares the club-face to the target. The momentum of his arm swing pulls his right foot onto its inner rim, and his right knee kicks in.

7 Stockton finishes with the majority of his weight on his front foot but he does leave some weight on his back foot, something he has always done. This idiosyncrasy of Stockton's swing can be problematic if overdone.

Jim Albus

Jim Albus was the first former club professional to win over $1 million on the Senior Tour. He worked in the New York area where he had an exceptional career at the club pro level. Playing in the highly competitive Metropolitan Section, he was four-time player of the year. In 1990 he left to join the Senior PGA Tour and had his first win by '91. He had a superb season in '94: two wins, six second places and $1.2 million in earnings. He won again in '95 and earned $750,000 more.

1 Jim Albus is a powerful man with moderate flexibility. To accommodate his large chest, he bends over more from his hips to create room for his arms to swing. If his posture were more upright, his chest would block his back-swing, forcing him to lift his arms and swing the club outside the target line.

Albus's wide stance creates stability for the lateral motion in his swing. His straight-legged appearance here is deceptive. During his pre-shot routine, he adds a bit more knee flex and shuffles his feet until his weight is evenly distributed from the balls of his feet to his heels. Once he is in perfect balance he pulls the trigger and starts his swing.

2 Albus begins his take-away by turning his left shoulder behind the ball which moves the club and his arms away as a unit to create a wide swing arc. As the take-away ends (when his hands pass his right foot) he cocks his wrists aggressively and creates maximum club-head elevation, eliminating the temptation to raise his arms past his limit of flexibility.

His goal is to keep the hands low but set the club-head in a high position. This keeps his swing short and under control, which is a necessity for players with bulky upper bodies. His aggressive wrist cock maximizes the power of leverage, while the short, connected arm swing will allow him to take advantage of his strong upper body later in the swing. His broadness limits the length of his back-swing but he further compensates for this by setting the club-shaft in a steep (vertical) position, creating additional height in the back-swing.

3 At the top of the back-swing the club swings to a three-quarter position with his hands still in front of his chest. Albus is in position to tuck his right elbow into his side and aggressively clear his left hip. This hand position gives him a very direct route to the ball, which is one reason he is such an accurate player.

4 At impact Albus has cleared his hips and his left arm is solidly connected to his chest. By keeping both feet nearly flat on the ground he keeps his right side in check on the down-swing, avoiding a lunge that would throw the club outside the target line. Note the white logo on the back of his shirt – it is almost in the exact position it was at address, indicating his chest waited during the down-swing for his arms to swing back in front of his body. This is a characteristic of all good swings and it is easy to ruin yours by rushing to turn your chest back to the ball. Good players have learned to wait, and so should you. Remember, the ball is not going anywhere until the club arrives, so do not turn your chest back to the ball too early.

5 Albus keeps his right side turning as the club continues to swing through on its way to the finish position. His right heel stays down and to the inside well after impact to keep the club tracking the target line.

6 Albus has fully rotated through the shot with his right shoulder closer to the target and almost all of his weight on his left side. You can check your own swing to see if you have achieved this powerful, full body release by tapping your right toe on the ground. If too much weight has been left behind you will have trouble with this task.

Hale Irwin

Irwin joined the PGA Tour in 1968. The highlights of his 20 career victories were his three US Open Championship titles. He earned the third at the age of 45, making him the oldest man ever to win the US Open. From early 1975 through 1978, he played 86 tournaments without missing a cut – the third best streak in Tour history. A five-time Ryder Cup Team member, Irwin joined the Senior PGA Tour in 1995 but also continued to play the PGA Tour. Although he played only 12 Senior events that year, he claimed two victories, and won twice more in 1996. In 1997 his full schedule earned him over $2 million on the Senior Tour for a record-shattering money title.

Irwin is one of the finest ball strikers ever to play the game. His effortless, energy-efficient swing has stood an enormous test of time. His continued elite level of play is not just a tribute to his mechanics, but also the rigorous fitness routine that has maintained his strength and flexibility.

1 At address he assumes excellent golf posture. The load bearing joints of his body are vertically aligned: The top of the spine, tip of the elbow, tip of the knee and balls of the feet.

This puts him in an ideal position to swing the club. His knees are just over his shoelaces not out over his toes; excess knee flex in place of hip bend will ruin your posture and your balance.

2 Irwin's one-piece take-away ends with a pronounced folding of his right elbow that sets the club-head well behind him. However, not all seniors are as supple as Irwin, nor do they have the slim upper body he has maintained throughout his career. Thus his build allows him to keep his right elbow pointing to the ground, a move that sets the club on plane. At this point in his swing, he has made a level hip turn, with the right hip serving as the pivot-point for his lower body.

3 At the top of the back-swing Irwin's shoulders are fully turned and his elbows are level. The club is supported by both hands and the club-face is in a square position – at the same angle as his left arm. The angle of his right arm matches his spine angle, indicating that he has maintained his golf posture. Both feet are flat on the ground with his upper body coiled against a resisting lower body.

4 The fullness of Irwin's shoulder turn is aided by the flare of the right foot. The more restricted your back-swing rotation, the more a flared right foot will increase your ability to turn behind the ball. As described in Chapter Two, an over-the-top move is allowed in the Senior Swing and a hint of it has always been evident at the start of Irwin's down-swing. His flared right foot, combined with a tucking of his right elbow, allow him to approach the ball from inside the target line. Note the level appearance of his hips at the top of the back-swing and the position of the left shoulder behind the ball. His lower body is anchored, with the upper body coiled against it.

5 Starting down, Irwin re-routes the club slightly out toward the target line when the right shoulder and hands move together just for an instant – but he returns the club to a perfect plane when the right elbow tucks into his right side. The left hip turns back over his left heel as his left arm slides down his chest for an inside approach to the ball.

6 Just after impact his arms are in front of his body because he keeps his head behind the ball creating a whip-like release of the stored energy. Notice how his left arm is against his chest, guaranteeing that the power generated by the rotation of his trunk and hips is transferred from his body to his arms and then into the golf ball.

7 Both arms are extended in a full release, and the butt of the club is pointed at the center of his body. This is because, while it turned, his upper body has also stayed back behind the ball, allowing the arms to release down the line.

8 He finishes in a balanced position, with his right shoulder closer to the target than his left, indicating that he has rotated his shoulders fully around his spine.

Graham Marsh

A native Australian, Graham Marsh turned professional in 1969 and has claimed 59 victories on five different circuits; he was in the Australian Order of Merit from 1978-1984. He joined the Senior PGA Tour in 1994 and has three victories. He entered 77 events, and finished in the top 10 in 37 of them and in the top 25 in 70. His 1996 statistics told the story: He ranked second in total driving, second in greens hit in regulation, fifth in scoring, fifth in birdies and ninth "all around".

1 Marsh creates a solid platform at address from which to execute his forceful swing. His feet are about shoulder-width apart, and both are flared to support the powerful motion of his lower body. Marsh bends from his hips so his arms can swing freely across the chest. This exemplary posture allows his arms to hang freely and his neck and shoulders to be free of tension. The club-face is aimed at the target, but his stance is slightly closed, which encourages a bigger shoulder turn and a wider swing arc.

2 Marsh starts the club back by swinging his left arm across his chest. As he does so you can see that his left arm is beginning to rotate by comparing his glove at address and in this frame. But it is one thing to allow the momentum of the arm swing to rotate the forearm and quite another to snatch the hands inside the toe line, taking the club-head out of position and robbing the swing of its width. There is no hint of the latter in Marsh's take-away.

When you take the club away like Marsh does, you will feel pressure begin to build in your right leg as the mass of your upper body turns behind the ball and your hips turn in response to the motion of your upper body. Regardless of how flexible you are, at this point in the swing your left foot should be firmly planted on the ground. You may let it rise later in the back-swing, but if it is up at this point, you have lost coil and ruined the path of the club.

3 Here the club-shaft and hands are perfectly positioned above the toe line, indicating a wide, powerful swing arc. With his lower body pivot-point established, his upper body can achieve maximum coil against the resistance of his lower body. To do so, Marsh turns his left shoulder behind the ball, and his right arm begins to fold.

4 At the top of his swing, Marsh has fully rotated his shoulders around his spine. His hands have maintained excellent extension from his body, adding width to the swing arc.

Marsh's left heel stays down, as it does for many of these top seniors, who are more flexible than the average person their age. If you are less supple, like for instance Jack Nicklaus, you can "let" your left heel come off the ground – but do not actively lift it.

5 Marsh begins the down-swing with a simultaneous movement of his left hip turning back over his left heel, the down-swing pivot-point, and his right elbow tucks into his right side and drops the club back on the shaft.

His lower body is in a dynamic, bow-legged position, providing a stable platform from which he will unleash its power through impact.

6 At impact his left hip has cleared. His left arm is against his chest and his head remains behind the ball. His right heel is down and rolled to the inside, keeping his hips and body level through the impact zone. Notice the back of his glove is in the same position it was at address, showing that the club-face is returned square to the target.

7 Marsh swings his arms past his body as his left hip turns over his left leg. This pulls his right heel off the ground but his head stays back, allowing the club to release fully. In another millisecond his head will rotate toward the target.

8 Marsh swings through to a balanced position with his knees together, hips facing the target, and his shoulders fully turned through, with his right shoulder closer to the target than his left shoulder.

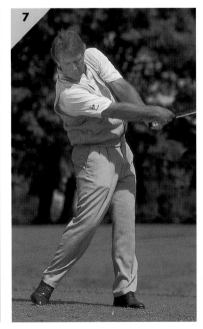

John Jacobs

John Jacobs is famed for his long-driving skill, winning over 100 Long Drive Championships. From 1968 to 1980, Jacobs was second five times on the PGA Tour. He joined the Senior PGA Tour in '88 and won fully exempt status with his second place at the '95 National Qualifying Tournament. In 1997, he finished in the top 10 twenty times with three second place finishes, earning him over $800,000 and a first place ranking in the driving distance, averaging over 290 yards per drive.

1 Jacobs is bent over just enough to create room for his arms to swing and hips to turn. For a large man with such a short swing, his stance is narrower than one might expect (see photo 5) but he has found the stance that fits his swing. He flares both feet and closes his stance: This lets him maximize his turn both back and through the ball and allows him to approach the ball from the inside on the down-swing.

2 Jacobs begins his back-swing with his lower body, as is evident by the distance his right pocket has already moved from its position at address. Both arms are extended as his shoulders and chest turn in the classic one-piece take-away used by so many long hitters. The club-shaft is parallel to his shoulder line, his right elbow is straight, and his wrists have yet to cock. There is no hint of any lifting of the club, a common power leak among amateurs.

3 As the club continues to swing back, the wrist cock begins, adding height to, and maintaining the width of the swing arc. It is this wrist action, coupled with a folding of his right elbow that sets the shaft in perfect position. Both knees have maintained their flex and his hips stay level as his upper body coils against the lower body.

4 Jacobs's right forearm is at the same angle as his spine at the top of his swing without straightening his posture. Unfortunately many senior players, trying for power, swing the arms too high. Because they exceed their flexibility, it forces them to "stand up" as they near the end of the back-swing. Jacobs exhibits our ideal top-of-the-swing-position for the Senior Swing – his hands are low but the club-head is high.

5 The completion of the back-swing is marked by a three-quarter position. His upper body is coiled over his resisting lower body. The key is that coil is a ratio: you do not need a 90 degree shoulder turn against a 45 degree hip turn. If you can only turn your shoulders 80 degrees you can create the same powerful coil simply by limiting your hip turn to 40 degrees. The ratio is the same and the result is the same: You stretch your muscles to produce power in your downswing.

6 Jacobs begins his down-swing with a lateral hip bump toward the target, and then his left hip turns forcefully behind him. Once the lateral move has shifted his weight to his left hip, he rotates his hips rather than continuing a lateral slide – a common error among amateurs. Simultaneously, Jacobs lets the club drop down into the delivery zone, with no effort to move the club toward the ball. His wrists are still cocked and waiting to release the club-head into the ball. The left hip is clear and the right side is in position to follow the club-head through the shot.

7 Through impact, Jacobs's head is behind the ball and his right foot is down and to the inside. If you push the right foot out toward the ball, it ruins both the path of the club-head and changes the swing plane – an error that leads to slices and pulls. The right heel can rise, but the foot itself must be rolling toward the target. Both arms are fully extended because of his right arm releasing through the hitting area.

8 He finishes in a balanced position in which the club has swung over his left shoulder and his right side has fully turned through the shot.

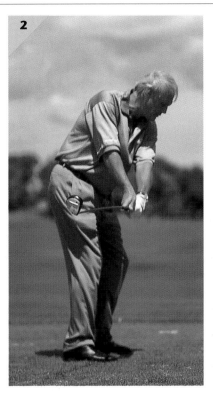

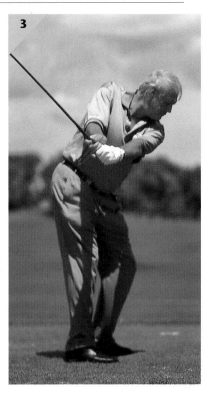

Jack Nicklaus

Beginning with brilliant play as an amateur, Nicklaus joined the PGA Tour in 1962, claiming his first victory at the US Open, defeating Arnold Palmer in a play-off. Over a span of almost 30 years he claimed 70 victories, including 20 Major Championships – a feat no other professional has come close to matching. His last Major Championship victory came at age 46 when he came from behind to win the 1986 Masters, providing fans with one of sport's greatest spectacles. Nicklaus became eligible for the Senior Tour in 1990 but played only four events – the Senior Tour's Majors – and again his record was remarkable. He won twice and finished second and third in the other two events. Through 1996, he played only 39 events on the Senior Tour but his success rate was vintage Nicklaus: 29 top-10 finishes and ten victories, eight of which were majors.

In his day, Jack Nicklaus had an awesome combination of power and accuracy, perhaps the straightest long driver that ever played the game. But, soon after he hit the PGA Tour, experts predicted his swing would not last because, with his arms so high above him on the back-swing by virtue of his flying right elbow, he had to make a very steep down-swing that was supposedly prone to produce off-center hits.

Jack Grout, his longtime teacher, taught the young Nicklaus three basic fundamentals: Hit the ball as hard as you can; "reach for the sky" with your arms and hands on the back-swing to produce the longest highest club-head arc you can; and keep your head still. Nicklaus followed these directions unequivocally so it is no wonder that his pre-1980 swing looked as it did – the one-piece take-away with a very late wrist cock that allowed the huge high arc; the massive body coil with the signature flying right elbow and the steep descent on the down-swing, fueled by a powerful leg drive.

In the prime of his life, Nicklaus dominated the world of golf, but by 1978-79, decreasing flexibility and his steep approach began to catch up with him. His shots lacked the old power and accuracy and it became apparent that something was wrong. After consulting with Grout, he realized that to maintain his world class form he must change his swing to suit the characteristics of his body better. The pictures here are from 1994 and show the result.

1 The Nicklaus pre-shot routine is legendary for its precision. He sights his target from behind the ball, visualizes the flight of the shot, walks aggressively to the ball and aims the club-face before he moves his body into position. Once he has the target in his sight, he starts his swing by swiveling his head to the right.

2 He has never deviated from his one-piece take-away, which creates a tremendously wide arc, evident by the distance the club-head is from his body.

3 In order to "reach for the sky" and keep his head still (Grout's fundamentals), Nicklaus let his right elbow fly. As a burly teenager with a large chest, he flew his elbow to compensate for his build. This pushed the club high above his body. Problems began when age decreased his hip speed and it could no longer compensate for the steep down-swing.

In 1979 he realized this and set about flattening his swing plane, but even though he has remained a great player, he has never quite regained his day in, day out dominance.

4 This is the only time in the swing where both arms should be fully extended. Nicklaus has great extension through the ball, in part because of his steady head. With his head as the axis, his arms fire the club-head at the target and the ball takes off for one heck of a ride.

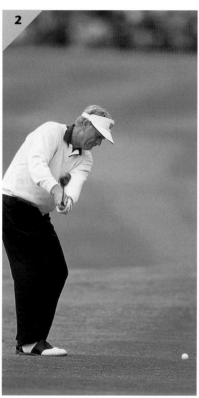

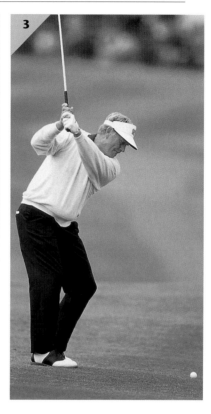

Even with an injured hip, Nicklaus still keeps his right side moving beautifully so that his body spirals up into a finish where his hands match the height they achieved in the back-swing.

5 Without question, Nicklaus's is still a young person's swing – high and arcing with very fast hips and a big leg drive – but unfortunately it is in an older man's body that is not as flexible as it once was. For most of his career, Nicklaus would aim down the left side of the fairway and, with his fast hips, bring the club-head to the ball with a slightly open face, producing a consistent high fade time after time.

But as his body changed and his hip speed slowed, so sometimes the club-head would arrive too soon, in a square or even closed position. This resulted in the dreaded "double-cross," where you aim left and the ball goes even further left.

In our opinion, Nicklaus would be even more dominant than he still is as a senior by dropping his right foot back a few inches, allowing his right arm to fold sooner, setting the club earlier and pushing it away from his chest. This would tuck his right elbow a touch and shallow his down-swing. It would also shorten his back-swing and make the angle of his left arm at the top of his swing much less vertical.

This assessment of even the great Jack Nicklaus makes the basic point: The process is the same for a high handicapper or champion. To play better golf as a senior you need to re-match how you swing the club to the current characteristics of your body.

Chapter seven

Equipment

Let's face up to it: having the correct equipment won't turn 36-handicappers into par-shooters, but using the right equipment can shave strokes off your score. More importantly, the clubs that fit your individual needs allow you to make your best possible golf swing and repeat it time after time. When you gain consistency in your swing, you will see consistency in your ball flight. In golf that means you know where the ball is going, and where it is not going. Having this arrow in your quiver will set you on a course to play your best golf.

When your equipment is matched to your individual needs, it becomes a compliment to your swing, freeing you to perform to your true potential. Research has shown that the ability to make a sound swing is directly dependent on having the correct club to swing. To maximize your performance in golf you should fit your golf clubs and golf ball to your own personal attributes, such as your physical characteristics. We don't have to remind you that, as a senior, these characteristics may have changed over the last decade or two. But, judging from the many seniors we see with misfit equipment, please keep in mind that it may be time to adjust, or even change, your weapons.

When you have poorly-fitted equipment, you will make compensations (errors) in your swing to adjust. For example, if you are using a club shaft that is too stiff – a common mistake in a senior's equipment – you will leave your weight on your right side during the down-swing to help the ball up in the air.

Inadvertently, you force yourself into a swing error to compensate for an inappropriate club specification. The golf swing can be difficult to master, but when you use the wrong equipment the task becomes almost impossible. Compensations are dangerous: first, because they're not easily repeatable, and second, because they usually rob you of power. These problems create a gruesome combination – inconsistent direction and a lack of distance.

Think of it logically. If correctly fitted equipment was important to your game when your athletic skills, such as eye-hand coordination and strength, were at their peak, how important is it now? The message is the same for all golfers, but it is especially important for seniors. Make sure that your equipment fits your body and golf swing.

The best way to do this is to find a PGA or an LPGA Teaching Professional who is skilled in club fitting. Your professional will take some static measurements indoors and then take you out to the range to watch your swing with your current equipment. You will be given a variety of clubs to try while the teacher/club fitter evaluates how the club affects your swing and your ball flight. Anything less is not a custom club fitting.

The specifications that have the most effect on your swing, and are therefore of primary importance to you as a golfer, are outlined in this chapter. If you decide to be custom-fitted for clubs, this information will help you participate in the process. If you decide to do fine tuning on your own, or aren't sure if you need to change equipment, this chapter will help with your choices.

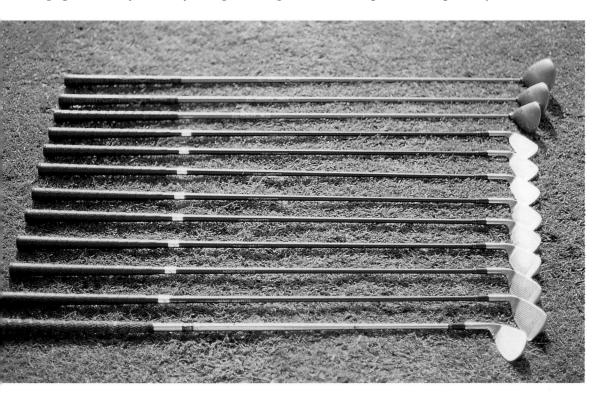

Even the best equipment won't turn you into Tom Weiskopf. But it might shave strokes off your score.

The right equipment can improve your golf swing and your scores.

Grips

Who's older, you or your grips?

If you have to think about that answer, your grips need to be replaced. Golf grips are by far the cheapest equipment change you can make and, judging from the thousands of folks we teach each year, most golfers need new grips. Grips age rapidly, not only because of use, but because of deterioration from the extreme temperatures they often suffer in car trunks. Also, unless you are conscientious about regularly cleaning them, dirt build-up makes even newer grips slick.

The problem is that worn and slick grips require a vise-like hold on the club and this wreaks havoc on a golf swing, especially if you are already struggling with distance. Employing the death grip makes a smooth take-away almost impossible. More likely the club is snatched away from the ball with not a hint of a "swing." To make matters worse, the effort required to control the club creates so much tension in the arms and hands, it is almost impossible for the wrists to hinge and unhinge effectively. For power, you need to create at least a 90-degree angle between your left arm and club-shaft during the back-swing but it won't happen if you squeeze the club to death. For a few dollars per club, new grips will solve these problems and add more than a few yards to every shot.

If your grips are less than a year old, keep them in top shape by washing them with

Worn grips can cause a multitude of swing errors and are easy and inexpensive to replace.

When a grip is the correct size for your hand, your middle fingers will lightly contact the thumb pad of your left hand.

warm, soapy water, then rinse and dry them. Grips more than a year or so old probably need to be replaced. If you are not sure, do a simple experiment. Go to your pro shop and pick a new club off the rack. If there's a discernible difference between the feel of this grip and those on your clubs, have yours replaced. There's no easier way to improve your golf swing.

The correct size grip

The correct grip size can improve your distance because it allows you to release the club properly through impact. A good release, the natural rotation of your right forearm over your left, means that you are delivering as much force to the ball as possible while still controlling the club. Too large a grip forces you to hold the club in the palms of your hands. Doing so restricts the release and causes the ball to fly right of the target. Too small a grip causes you to overuse or "flip" your hands through impact and the ball flies left of your target.

You will know the grip size is correct when the tip of your left hand ring finger and index finger lightly contact the thumb pad of your left hand, but be sure you are gripping the club properly as outlined in Chapter One. If there is a large gap, then your grips are too big. Conversely, if one or more of your fingers is digging into your heel pad your grips are too small.

Oversized grips

Many seniors automatically turn to oversized or jumbo grips but, unless you suffer from arthritis and can't curl your fingers around a proper size grip, a jumbo grip is a big mistake for seniors. Ben Hogan used oversized grips (not the jumbo version) to help cure his hook, but most golfers fight a slice and too large a grip compounds their problems.

If you do suffer from arthritis in your hands, see Chapter 3 for special grip and swing adjustments.

Oversized grips force a player to hold the club too much in the palms of the hands. This translates into swing errors, the most damaging of which is restricted wrist action.

Shaft flex

Load versus
club-head speed

Don't be fooled by the fact that you still feel as strong as you felt in your thirties and forties. Strength diminishes gradually over the course of a lifetime, but flexibility can diminish sooner and decline rapidly. Because you still feel strong, you may think you can use the same clubs, especially since your swing speed remains unchanged. Club-head velocity is no longer the only standard for determining shaft flex. What matters is where you load and unload the shaft and this relates to your flexibility and your strength. If your swing is shorter because you are less flexible, you will load and unload the club shaft differently to the way you did in the past. In this case a more flexible shaft may be right for you.

Where and how much the shaft flexes during your swing determines the club-face position at impact. If the shaft is too flexible, the excessive bending makes it hard to square the club-face at impact. If it is too stiff, it won't bend much at all. This means you will get little whip out of the shaft at impact and the club-face will arrive open to the target line, resulting in weak shots to the right.

Generally, most senior golfers use too stiff a shaft. Your goal should be to swing the most flexible shaft you can, without the ball flying left and right of your target with no predictable pattern. If your shots are flying low and to the right, your shafts are too stiff. The more flexible the shaft the higher the ball will fly, and most seniors could benefit from a higher ball flight.

Though the shaft is straight at address it should flex, or bend, during your down-swing.

Longer shafts and oversized club-heads

Longer shafts and oversized club-heads can be a great benefit to golfers who have lost some distance. All else being equal, a longer shaft swings the club-head on a wider arc and this translates into greater swing speed at impact, adding yardage to your shots. The larger head gives you an expanded hitting surface and a more forgiving sweet spot, increasing the chance for solid contact.

Unless you are an expert player who likes to vary your ball flight on command – low draw, high fade, etc. – there's not much to dislike about oversized club-heads. It is not just hype. Oversized club-heads can improve your game. However, longer shafts are a trickier equipment issue. True, a longer swing arc can mean increased distance, but it has to be combined with solid contact. Sadly, the longer the arc, the more difficult it becomes to make solid contact. At some stage, making the shaft longer reaches the point of diminishing returns. You may well have a longer swing arc and increased club-head speed, but if your contact is poor – out on the toe of the club for instance – you will find you actually lose yardage rather than gain it.

The only way to determine how long you can go is to hit clubs of varying lengths and compare. Besides feel, you can use impact tape, powder, or chalk to determine the "centeredness" of hit for each swing. To find out which length is right for you, tape or

Clubs with longer than standard shafts increase club-head speed to add distance to your game.

Drivers used to be about 43 inches with approximately 11 degrees of loft. Today, lighter shaft materials have made possible exceptionally long driver shafts. Studies show that if you lengthen the club-shaft in your driver by two inches you can add about 4 miles per hour to your swing speed, which translates into about 12 yards of additional distance. There are two problems, however. First, it is tricky simply extending the length of your current driver, because when you change one specification of a club, it affects the others. Second, the ability to make a solid contact, another distance essential, may be reduced.

Swing speed

Club speed is the velocity of the club-head as it passes through the 4 inches just preceding the ball. For every 1 mile an hour that you increase your club-head speed, you can generate about 3 more yards in the distance the ball will travel.

Perimeter weighted clubs have a cavity in the back of the club-head created by taking weight from the center of the club-head and distributing it around the perimeter. This reduces twisting when contact is away from the sweet spot, and so it minimizes the distance and directional loss. Off-center hits also feel softer and transmit less vibration, another plus for seniors who have tender or aching joints. This expanded sweet spot is the secret of oversize club-heads, and materials like titanium make perimeter weighting more effective. The lightness and strength of titanium allows the club manufacturers a greater versatility in shifting the weight around the club-head and also increasing its overall size. The standard stainless steel head weighs about 200 grams, while the titanium version is a mere 120 grams. Therefore the club maker using titanium has 80 additional grams to make game improvement changes such as super-sized club-heads and extreme perimeter weight to keep your drives flying straight.

Longer shafts and oversized club-heads *continued*

Oversized club-heads offer a larger sweet spot to negate the effects of off-center hits.

powder each club-face and try out three different shaft lengths, hitting 10 shots with each length on two separate occasions. As soon as your number of off-center hits is greater than 30 percent, the shaft is too long.

Shaft length in general

For all your clubs, it is important that the shaft length be correct. When shafts are too long or short it affects your golf posture by setting your body out of balance before you swing. The problem gets worse once the club is set in motion. If your clubs are too long you will compensate by standing too erect. In doing so, your weight gets back on your heels and your arms can't hang freely. When your clubs are too short, you bend over too much, forcing your weight onto your toes. If your clubs are too short and you make a good swing, you will make contact with the ball on the toe. If your clubs are too long, your contact will be in by the heel.

Weight

The weight of a golf club is expressed in two measurements: ideal weight and swing weight. The total weight of the golf club is the actual scale weight or "ideal weight," for

A club fitter can measure the "swing weight" of your clubs on a specially designed scale.

example 13 ounces. It is important because, if your club is too heavy for you, you will lose control of the club and disrupt your swing; if it is too light, you can't feel the club-head and your timing will be poor.

The "swing weight" is the relationship between the length of the club and the amount of weight in the club-head. How the weight is distributed determines the "feel" of the club-head. The swing weight should be the same for all your clubs, so that the overall feel is consistent, but the scale weight differs from club to club, with your sand-wedge being the heaviest. For senior golfers, both scale weight and swing weight should get lighter as you get older.

Over all, the best way to determine what clubs are right for you is the "hit 'em and fit 'em" technique, in other words, be fitted by an expert who will give you a broad selection of clubs to swing.

Lie angle

Lie angle is determined by the angle the shaft creates with the ground when your club is soled at address. Though a club fitter judges lie angle dynamically by taping the sole of your club and having you hit off a special board, you can in fact make a rudimentary judgment of your own by observing your club-head at address.

Assuming you are standing in correct golf posture, if the toe of your club is up in the

Longer shafts and oversized club-heads *continued*

When your clubs have the correct lie angle you will be able to set the sole of the club flush with the ground.

If your clubs are set at the wrong lie angle you won't be able to set the sole of the club flush with the ground. The club is too upright for the player, which forces him to compensate by flattening the shaft. This creates yet another error because it puts the toe in the air, which will cause the ball to fly to the left. Only a club repair-man can make the proper repair by bending the club at the hosel so the club sits flush to the ground.

air, your clubs are too upright for you and, without swing compensations, the ball will fly to the left. A club technician will flatten your clubs by increasing the angle between the shaft and the club-head, thereby dropping the toe down to the ground. If the heel of the club is up in the air, your clubs are too flat for you, in which case the opposite repair will be made: decrease the angle between the shaft and club-head so the club can sit flush to the ground.

Loft angle

The non-technical description of loft is how much your club-face looks at the sky and it obviously has a major effect on the height and trajectory of a shot. It is difficult to make a well-balanced swing with too little loft on your clubs because you will subconsciously make adjustments to help the ball in the air. Too much loft costs you distance and encourages an over-swing.

Adjusting loft from the normal is called strengthening or weakening. If a club-maker strengthens a pitching-wedge, i.e. changes it from say 56 degrees of loft to 54, you will hit the ball lower and a bit longer. Weakening is the opposite adjustment and is used to raise the trajectory.

The loft of a club is the angle of the club-face, or how much the club-face is angled toward the sky.

Graphite *or steel*

Golf clubs have come a long way from their original wooden shafts. Today, graphite and other light-weight materials have made it possible for manufacturers to move more weight into the club-head for higher, more powerful shots. Steel shafts are less expensive, and better players sometimes prefer them, because they produce more accurate shots. But if distance is your problem and money isn't, go for the graphite or titanium. If you have arthritis in the joints of your hands and arms, you will definitely appreciate graphite's softer feel at impact.

Offset heads

Irons, and more recently woods, are offered in an "offset" style where the leading edge of the club is behind, or offset from, the hosel. This feature helps to get the ball in the air more easily. If you are a low ball hitter, you may want to give these clubs a test drive. If you already hit the ball high, stick with the standard design.

The right putter for you

You should match your putter to your current skill level, but the choice is mostly a matter of personal preference.

Putters are made in three basic styles: the box, the blade, and the mallet. The box putter features perimeter weighting which gives you a bigger sweet spot and, therefore, more margin for error in off-center contact. Blade putters, preferred by golfers with very consistent putting strokes, have most of their weight in the center of the club-face. Therefore mis-hits are more likely to roll off line, but centered hits roll straight and true. The mallet putter often features a heavy head. Seniors, who struggle with excess hand motion and have short, abrupt putting strokes, will find that the weight of the

The long putter can be especially useful for those who feel they've lost the rhythm of their putting stroke.

mallet keeps the club-head swinging with more of a "stroking" motion. Mallets are also helpful on slow greens because the weight of the head tends to roll the ball firmly.

The long putter

Pendulum putters, featuring a shaft that extends about chest high, can be found with every variety of club-head. Since you can anchor the top of the long shaft against your chest with your left hand and move it with your right hand, the senior golfer who struggles with excessive wrist action can find relief with this style of putter. These putters tend to be especially good on short putts, because the stroke is very stable, but on long putts you may have difficulty with distance control. The key to the long putter is patience, because it takes about two weeks of practice to develop a feel for it. But once you do, it can be very effective.

Choosing the right ball

Golf balls come with basically two types of covers: surlyn, a hard material, and balata, a softer material. The average golfer chooses surlyn for its durability, that is, the cover won't cut if you hit the ball with the leading edge of the club. Expert players prefer balata because its high spin rate – the rate it spins around its axis – allows them to curve and spin the ball on command and its soft feel gives them greater touch around the greens.

Ball construction

Two-piece balls have solid interiors and an outer cover, while three-piece balls have a liquid core surrounded by a rubber winding, and then covered by either a balata or surlyn case. If you are looking for distance, use a two-piece ball with a low spin rate, which will also minimize slices and hooks by reducing side spin.

With the introduction of lithium surlyn, a softer cover that gives you more feel and a high spin rate, the playing difference between three and two-piece designs have narrowed considerably. Increasingly golfers choose their balls on the basis of spin rate.

For control and maneuverability, choose a ball with a high spin rate and a soft cover. If you want maximum distance and a durable golf ball that flies higher and gets more roll, choose a two-piece hard cover ball with a low spin rate. For a blend of distance and control, opt for a combination, a moderate spin rate with a durable cover.

Dimple *arrangement*

Back in the early days golfers learned that, if they scuffed up a ball, it had a tendency to fly better. That was the beginning of the quest for the perfect dimple pattern. The key elements are the depth, the diameter, the number and the shape of the dimples. Manufacturers create different trajectories, distances, and spin rates by making adjustments to the dimple pattern, but it is up to you to match your skill level to the pattern.

Testing *golf balls*

Manufacturers work within certain specifications, based on the Rules of Golf, as they develop new advances in golf ball technology. Their testing machines are set to approximate a Tour Pro's swing speed of 109 miles per hour with a driver. Carry plus roll of a ball struck by these machines may not exceed 296.8 yards. By comparison, the average golfer has a swing speed of between 70 and 90 miles per hour and drives that travel 180 to 220 yards.

Your secret weapons — utility woods

Utility woods used to be thought of as a crutch for short hitters. But LPGA Tour Players, who tackle courses between 6100 and 6400 yards (the same distance most male amateurs play from) have long known the advantage utility woods give them over long irons.

On the Senior Tour, several great players of today and yesterday have made the smart choice and added some utility woods to their golf bags. Can Chi Chi Rodriguez, Lee Trevino and Orville Moody still hit a perfect 3-iron? You bet they can, but they know that a 5-wood and a 7-wood make their lives easier and make them more competitive. Even the King, the great Arnold Palmer, has been known to carry a 5-wood!

Utility woods are fast replacing long irons in the smart golfer's bag.

A sound golf swing and the right equipment are a powerful combination for maximizing your potential as a golfer. With this basic rule in mind, we firmly recommend that you include an assortment of utility woods in your set. Utility woods, the 5, 7, 9 and even 11-wood, are fast replacing long irons in the smart golfer's bag.

There's no mistaking that advances in design make utility woods easier to hit from a wide range of lies. They have soles that are specially designed to make the club skim over a tight lie on the one hand and cut through heavy rough on the other. Also, the hosels are often designed so they won't get caught in high grasses which, with a conventional iron, would cause the club-face to twist before impact.

The real secret of the newer utility woods is the combination of the length of the shaft and the loft of the club-face. As an experienced golfer, you know that a club's distance potential is a function of its shaft length and face loft. A driver produces the most distance because it has the longest shaft and the least loft. Similarly, a 3-iron produces more distance than a 9-iron because its shaft is longer and its face has less loft than a 9-iron. But a 3-iron is also difficult to hit off the ground because it has so little loft. The

Utility woods are easier to hit than long irons and send the ball on a much higher trajectory.

Your secret weapons – utility woods *continued*

corresponding utility wood, a 7 in this case, has a longer shaft combined with more loft, producing the same distance but making it easier to hit. If you don't hit the ball very high you will appreciate the additional loft a utility wood offers. So if you had trouble with the long irons as a "junior" there's simply no reason to continue the struggle. Utility woods are the right choice for almost every golfer, especially seniors.

Bounce, the bulged shape of the sole of a wedge, prevents the club from digging into sand or heavy rough.

The wedges

You can save strokes if you choose your wedges correctly.

The performance of a wedge is strongly influenced by the design of the sole of the club, specifically its bounce. Bounce, the protrusion on the sole of a wedge, is what makes the club effective in deflecting (bouncing) off a surface of grass, sand or dirt at impact. The greater the bounce, that is to say the further the sole extends below the leading edge, the less likely it is that the club-head will dig into the ground.

A pitching-wedge with 50 degrees of loft and about 4 degrees of bounce works well from tight lies and from the fairway. The average sand-wedge has around 56 degrees loft with 11 degrees bounce to prevent the leading edge from digging into the sand. It works well in soft sand and around the greens in normal green-side rough.

The lob wedge has between 60 and 64 degrees of loft with a small amount of bounce. It works well from wet, hard sand or hardpan and, with its extra loft, it can get the ball up in a hurry so that it lands softly from a tight lie.

It is not unheard of to carry a fourth wedge, especially if you face short pitches from tight, closely-mowed fairways where you need a wedge with little bounce. It can also be useful as a "gap" wedge when you have a large gap between the distance you hit

your pitching- and sand-wedges. In other words, if you hit your pitching-wedge 100 yards and your full sand-wedge only 70 yards, the gap is 30 yards. This can be a problem because it will force you either to modify your pitching-wedge swing or swing too hard with your sand-wedge. A fourth wedge, with loft and shaft length between that of your pitching- and sand-wedges, can help you at in-between distances by allowing you a full swing rather than a modified one.

If your bag can't accommodate a fourth wedge, another solution to the problem of this gap is to lengthen the shaft of your sand-wedge and/or decrease its loft. This increases

Wedges comes in a variety of lofts. Many players, including experts, have added diversity to their short games by carrying three wedges in their bag.

its overall distance potential with a full swing and then, by simply gripping it down an inch or two, you can hit it about 10 yards shorter when you need to.

In the bunker, you can save some strokes by matching your sand-wedge system to the texture of the sand. When it is soft and fluffy use a wedge with a lot of bounce. When the sand is hard, wet or crusty, select a wedge with minimal bounce.

Chapter eight

Fitness

It's never too late

When it comes to getting in "golf shape," it is never too late to start. Studies show that age is not the insurmountable barrier to a person's physical performance that it was once thought to be. Michael Pollock, an exercise physiologist at the University of Florida who studies elite older athletes, says your physical ability depends not so much on your age as on whether or not you adhere to an exercise routine.

Dr. Pollack's studies reveal that losing muscle mass is not inevitable. "Athletes who only ran kept their hearts and legs fit, but the rest of them withered away." Weight training helps solve that problem. You can start exercising at any age and will see improvement. With the right program you can increase not only your endurance and strength, but you will lose fat and increase bone density, which helps protect you against the danger of brittle bones associated with old age.

In the early 1970s, Dr. Pollock began monitoring men between the ages of 50 and 82, then followed them for the next two decades. He reports: "This study, as well as others, has shown that age is not a determining factor. After ten years," Pollock says "the people that continued to train in exactly the same way didn't lose any aerobic capacity at all. The ones that reduced their

Senior PGA Tour star Bruce Crampton's dedication to fitness has kept his playing skills at an elite level for many years.

training – usually it was in intensity, because that's the hardest thing to keep up – lost about 10 percent for that decade."

In the next decade, they lost a little more, but were still in the top 5 percent – not for their age group, but for the entire population. Their risk factors for heart disease and diabetes were also low. Athletes who started training with conditions such as erratic heartbeats found the problem did not worsen with age as one might have expected.

Fitness includes flexibility

Ron Peyton, a physical therapist who served as a sports medicine consultant during the 1996 Olympics, knows that older golfers are ill-prepared for the rigors of golf. "It's no wonder they get hurt," says Peyton. "The golf swing involves an extreme amount of bending and twisting of the spine, as well as

Injury prevention

The American Physical Therapy Association has some advice on how to prevent injuries:

■ Get to the course 15 minutes early and stretch your back, shoulders, and legs.

■ Walk the course instead of riding in a cart. If carts are mandatory, rotate the chore with your riding companion.

■ On cool days, layer your clothes to trap body heat.

■ Start your practice sessions with a 9-iron and work up to a 5-iron before using a driver.

■ Stop playing immediately if your swing is restricted by pain.

■ Lift clubs and baggage out of the car in a way that prevents back pain.

■ If you get hurt, see a physician or physical therapist who can prescribe a stretching and strengthening program.

rotation of the hips and shoulders. The lower back and neck are injured the most. When there is a lack of flexibility, stress is placed on these areas and that will eventually lead to permanent damage."

Warming up before exercise helps a gradual increase of muscle tension and decreases the possibility of an injury, mainly because it raises the body's core temperature, allowing muscles to stretch more easily.

Golf and exercise

With the exception of Sam Snead, Gary Player, Arnold Palmer, and a few other professionals, golfers traditionally have not been perceived as well-conditioned athletes. Subscribers to that theory argue that, since golf does not call for running, jumping, or lifting heavy loads, there is little need for strength enhancement programs. "These perceptions," says Dr. Frank Jobe, the Director of the Centinela Hospital's Fitness Institute, "are now changing, reflecting a growing awareness by amateurs and pros alike that a specific program of stretching and strengthening exercises will not only lower the risk of injury, but will improve performance at every level."

Dr. Jobe and his colleagues at the Centinela Hospital Sports Medicine Center have conducted perhaps the most extensive and influential research to date using electromyography to identify the most active muscles during the golf swing. The findings are summarized below:

■ Your golf swing is two-sided, so you should strengthen the muscles on both sides of your body equally.

■ Since your hips supply the major source of power on the down-swing, concentrate on developing your thigh and hip muscles.

■ Your ability to rotate around the fixed axis of your spine is critical to generating coil during your swing. Stretching exercises will preserve

your rotational flexibility, and exercising your back muscles will give you the stability you need to coil.

■ The rotator cuff muscles in your shoulders require special exercises because they are the most active of all your upper body muscles.

It is the opinion of almost every fitness expert that all senior golfers should be on a golf-specific exercise program, unless their physicians advise them otherwise. This advice has been already heeded by a number of professional golfers. On the Senior Tour, players like Bruce Crampton, Bob Charles, and, of course, Gary Player, show the sleekness and longevity attributable to a regular exercise program.

What about you?

Why should you work out? The message from both the laboratory and practical experience is clear – the stronger your muscles,

PGA and Senior Tour veteran Gary Player attributes much of his spectacular success in golf as both a "junior" and senior pro to his life-long dedication to fitness.

the greater the pulling force, and so the harder and faster you can swing the club. Further, the stronger your golf-related muscles are, the better able you are to hold your body in the positions required during the golf swing. This means that, over time, you will hit the ball more solidly and, therefore, farther.

Neuro-physiological research proves that strength training not only makes your muscles stronger and larger, it also makes them more efficient. This increase in efficiency is the reason you will experience an immediate jump in your strength level after beginning a fitness program. Biomechanics expert Mike Ploski explains, "A major part of building strength is your brain activating the muscle. When you work a certain muscle, even with a light weight, the brain targets that muscle, and during the contraction, it recruits more fibers so that the pull force increases. Because of this neural factor, you don't have to wait months to see positive results."

It is very important for all readers of this book to remember, however, that before attempting any of the exercises shown here or following any of the other recommendations in this book, they should always have their physician's approval first.

How strong do you need to be?

This is not a book on health or physical conditioning. It is a guide to better golf, so

How muscles
grow

The strength of a well-nourished muscle is related to its cross sectional area. When you put load or stress on the muscle fibers in the correct way, they break down and re-knit, getting bigger and thicker – a process known as hypertrophy. If you give muscles time to repair themselves after you work out, they can grow broader and stronger. Stronger muscles improve your balance and equilibrium. They allow you to do more work, to overcome more resistance, and to swing a club faster. A strong muscle is a fast muscle. A tired muscle is a slow muscle.

Golf and exercise *continued*

PGA and Senior Tour veteran Tom Weiskopf is "golf strong."

In this book, when we refer to strength and flexibility, it is in relation to golf. Strength is a relative term depending on the sport. Are PGA Tour professionals Ben Crenshaw or Jeff Sluman stronger than top basketball player Shaquille O'Neal? In the weight room, no. In relation to their ability to generate distance in the golf swing however, yes.

Abundant strength is good for a golf swing, as long as it comes with flexibility. However, in golf, you reach a point of diminishing returns because you only need to be "so strong." For instance, all else being equal, a tour player who hits the ball 260 yards off the tee is worse off than a player who hits the same shot 310 yards (a difference of 50 yards), but 260 yards is good enough to make the player competitive. Yet if that player could only hit the ball 230 yards versus 260 (a difference of only 30 yards), he probably would not be long enough to play the tour. This threshold of distance works the same way for the senior player. On one side of threshold you are long enough, and on the other you are too short. Everyone's threshold is different, but you need to make sure your training program keeps you on the right side of the too short/strong enough divide.

our recommendations are made only with golf in mind. Sport-specific training is fast becoming the norm and it is obvious that you don't prepare your body for a marathon the same way you do for a 100-yard sprint.

Golf strong

So golf strength, the ability to control the club and produce distance with accuracy, is not the same as having general strength, the kind that lifts heavy loads. Tom Weiskopf, a big man who is still a competitive player on the Senior Tour, admits that in the weight room he can't bench-press 150 pounds, but he can out-drive the vast majority of those who can.

Being golf strong involves more than just muscle power. It is a combination of factors, including the quality of your golf swing, the length of your arms, the condition of your golf muscles, your flexibility, your ratio of slow-twitch to fast-twitch muscle fibers, the fit of your equipment, your overall fitness, and your mental approach – are you wired to be a big hitter? In the next section of this chapter you will learn the golf-specific exercises to increase your strength and flexibility.

Things you should know about working out

There are many opinions about structuring a golf-specific exercise program, but some basics are consistent in all theories. To maximize your distance, your golf-specific training program must include weight training, though it is neither necessary nor advisable to strain yourself with heavy weights or spend an inordinate amount of your time in a gym.

Like the mental side of playing golf, there is also a mental aspect of physical fitness that you can use to your advantage. When you use weights, repeat affirmations such as,

"This lift is for power. I am getting stronger. This increases the length of my drives." During the exercise, you should also visualize the specific muscle getting stronger. When you contract a muscle, hold the position for several counts and visualize the muscle growing in size and strength. After each set, you should swing a golf club, or simulate the motion, focusing on the muscles that you just worked. This alerts the brain, telling it "Hey, this muscle group is important, make it grow."

Be sure to reject the misguided notion of "no pain, no gain." You can achieve a high level of fitness without causing yourself any pain. Pain is a warning sign, especially if you have a pre-existing condition like golfer's elbow (see Chapter 3). The simple rule is: if it hurts, stop!

Work out regularly

Research has shown that if you stop working out, your capabilities are significantly diminished within two to four weeks. However, once you've established your level of fitness – whatever that might be – you can maintain your strength gains and reduce the frequency of your work-outs by 30 to 66 percent without losing conditioning – if you maintain the intensity of each work-out. Another key, with any exercise program, is the regularity with which you do it. A little done on a regular basis is better than a lot

The best time to exercise is when you want to. Some people are morning people, while others are afternoon or evening people. Choosing one time of day rather than another does not make the work-out any more or less effective. What is important is that you pick a time when you are most likely to fulfill your commitment. If you are not a morning person, for instance, and you schedule a morning work-out, you will find yourself tempted to skip it entirely. That is when time of day really does make a difference.

Golf and exercise *continued*

done every once in a while. So work out three times a week to start and then, when you reach your desired level of fitness, you can (if you want to) go on a maintenance program by working out twice a week. Remember to maintain the intensity of each work-out, though, to keep your level of fitness.

Use light weights and high repetitions

As a golfer, your goal is to build the strength necessary for fast, explosive movements. Even though each person is born with a certain ratio of speed-to-endurance muscle fibers, you can increase the efficiency of the speed fibers you have by using an amount of weight that allows you to perform the same exercise at least 12 times in a row. Start, if you can, by using 50 percent of the heaviest weight that you are capable of lifting once. For example, if you can bench press 90 pounds, start with 45 pounds and do three sets of 12 repetitions. Repetitions (reps) are the number of times in succession you perform an exercise before taking a rest. A set is one series of repetitions, and you should do 2 to 4 sets, resting 60 to 90 seconds between each set. If you can't get this far with the weights at 50 percent of maximum, then you should cut down the amount of weight, not the number of sets or repetitions. When you can do all the sets in good form, with mini-

mal effort, you are ready gradually to increase the weight.

The ideal amount of weight for any given exercise should exhaust the muscle sufficiently so that it is incapable of performing the last two or three reps of the last set.

Since muscles exert only a pull force on your bones and joints – they can't push – some muscles involved in movement exist in pairs to ensure your body has the full range of motion. For example, the triceps muscle pulls (extends) the arm straight, while the biceps pulls (flexes) it back. Your triceps are important in your golf swing and your biceps are less so, yet to preserve your coordination, you must work both the muscle and its partner.

Stretch out regularly

While your muscular strength declines relatively slowly over your lifetime, your flexibility can diminish quickly. Therefore, your fitness routine should combine a weight program with regular stretching. You don't have to worry about getting "muscle bound" – if you work your muscles correctly through their full range of motion, strong muscles will also be flexible muscles. Becoming muscle-bound results from improper training technique, not the training itself. In fact, correct use of weights increases flexibility. So always work with the correct amount of weight and concentrate on the form of the exercise.

The pre-game warm-up

The windmill

Stand with your feet shoulder width apart and extend your arms as if they were wings, level to the ground (see photo 1). Make sure your arms are no higher than shoulder level. Slowly rotate your arms clockwise in a small circle, keeping your shoulders as still as possible. After ten revolutions, stop and reverse the circle in a counter-clockwise direction.

The cane

Using a 5-iron, extend your arms in front of you, resting your hands on the grip end of the handle. Keeping your arms extended, bend your knees until you are in a squatting position (see photo 2), then rise to your full height. Repeat ten times.

Torso stretch

Place a club behind your shoulders and loop your arms over the shaft. Simulate a gentle slow motion golf swing by turning into your back-swing and follow-through (see photo 3). Repeat five times.

Jack Nicklaus began a weight-training program at age 52 in order to preserve his competitiveness. In typical Nicklaus style, he analyzed his problem (losing distance with his driver), and realized that if he was to remain competitive, he would have to work with weights. In addition to his stretching program, he works with light weights through high repetitions.

The pre-game warm-up *continued*

Baseball to golf

Stand upright and make a few practice swings, as though you were hitting a waist-high pitch in baseball (see photo 4). Keeping the motion continuous, slowly incline your spine toward your normal full swing position until you are clipping the grass. Repeat five times.

4

Golf specific work-out program

The author, Dr. T.J. Tomasi and his fellow PGA Golf Professional, Bruce Adams, (see photo 5) are 57 and 70 years old respectively. They have limited the effects of aging and kept their swings in good shape with a life-long commitment to physical fitness and demonstrate each exercise in this program.

The cost of the "home gym" shown in the following photos is modest. Of course, it is best to go to a fully equipped gym that features sophisticated weight training and cardiovascular conditioning equipment, with fitness counselors to assist you. But if time, convenience and/or money are factors, the exercises outlined below will suffice to make you golf fit.

Flexibility program

Palm-to-cheek stretch

This exercise requires no equipment, it works all the muscles you use in the golf swing and it actually simulates a golf swing. Because it is so easy to do, you can and should do it many times a day – on the course, watching TV or at the office. If you make it a habit to do this exercise during your normal daily routines, you will develop one of the most important attributes necessary to play better golf – flexibility.

To begin, stand with both arms stretched out in front of you. Reach under your left arm and curl your right wrist behind your left elbow. Keeping this relationship, slowly place your right palm on the right side of your face. This will stretch your left side muscles – especially your rotators – so do it gently. If you can't reach far enough to lay your palm flat against your cheek, put it on your chin.

Now, with your left arm straight, bend from your hip joints into your golf posture, just as if you were about to make a swing with your 5-iron (see photo 1 on page 124). Imagine there is a club in your left hand. Using a slow motion back-swing, swing the imaginary club

Flexibility program *continued*

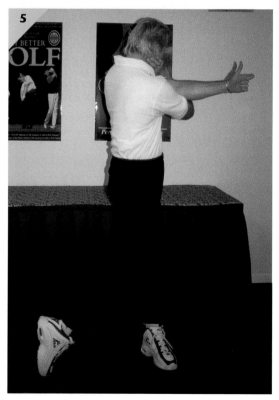

to the top of your swing (see photo 2).

In photos 1 and 2, notice the model's head is obscuring the lower left portion of the picture behind him. In photo 2, the top of the swing position, his head has floated to the right until it is located over his right foot. This is an appropriate motion for the Senior Swing, where the head and top of the spine must be allowed to move.

In photo 2 you can see the coil created between the upper and lower body. This is an essential part of the exercise, as it is for the golf swing. The creases in the model's shirt are a clear indication of coil, and not a lack of ironing skill. You can also see the lattissimus dorsi, one of the largest and most powerful muscles in your body for golfing, protruding below the shoulder. This is an important golf muscle which you will learn how to develop in the strength training section.

Hold this coiled position (photo 2) for at least 20 seconds, without bouncing or straightening out of your golf posture. Now start your down-swing slowly and stop with your left arm parallel to the ground (photo 3). Hold this position for a count of 20. Remember to let your head move back toward its address position, not past it, and make sure to shift your weight and turn your hips, just as you would in a regular swing. This will maintain the stretch all the way though impact (photo 4). As you move up into your follow-through, let your head be pushed up by your right shoulder while you keep your left arm straight and your right palm in place (photo 5). While it may not appear so, this is a maximum stretch position that works the right side of your upper body as well as it did the left.

Hip stretch

Sit with your back straight and one foot flat on the floor. Place the ankle of your other foot over your knee so that your folded leg forms a 90-degree angle. Anchor your ankle with your hand so that it does not move out of place, but do not pull on your foot during the exercise. Place your other hand on the folded knee and exert a gentle push on the knee, moving it slightly down toward the ground (see photo 6). Relax the pressure and then repeat it, increasing it until you feel the

Flexibility program *continued*

stretch in your hip. Hold for 30 seconds, then switch legs to work your other hip.

The body hang

Stand erect with your feet shoulder width apart and bend from your hip joints, placing your hands on your knees. Pause in this position for several seconds, to let your back stretch out, then take one hand off and let it hang on its own. Hold for several seconds, then take the other hand off so that your upper body weight pulls you toward the ground (see photo 7). Hang in this position for about 30 seconds, then before you straighten up, replace your hands on your knees and use them to push off as you regain your standing position. This will take

any sudden strain off your lower back. Repeat at least twice.

Be especially careful not to lock your legs at any point – always do this exercise with a light to moderate bend at the knees.

Bent leg stretch

Sit on the floor with both legs extended and your back straight. Fold one leg under the other and keep the top leg slightly bent at the knee. Without any sudden bending, reach toward the toes of your extended leg (see photo 8). When you reach your limit, stop and hold the position for 15 seconds. Do three repetitions and then switch legs. When you stretch forward to touch your toes, try to keep your shoulders from hunching.

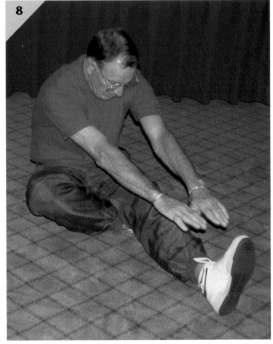

The reverse knee stretch

Lay on your right side, and cross your right ankle over your left leg in order to anchor it and provide resistance. Wrap your arm around your knee and slowly pull your right knee to your chest, keeping it in its locked position over your left leg (see photo 9). Hold for 30 seconds and then reverse the position so you work your other hip.

Knee tuck stretch

Lay on your back with your legs and shoulders flat on the floor, raise your legs straight up and then fold them onto your chest. Wrap your

arms around your knees and hold for 30 seconds (see photo 10). Repeat three times. The knee tuck stretch is really two exercises in one: lifting your legs straight up works your abdominals; folding your knees onto your chest stretches the muscles in your lower back.

Shoulder stretch

Lay on your left side with your legs bent at 90-degrees. Place your left arm over your right thigh to secure your legs in place so they will not move as you stretch. Once in position, extend your right arm fully and let gravity pull your arm down until it is close to or touching the floor (see photo 11). Hold for 15 seconds and then switch sides.

Flexibility program *continued*

The cross-leg stretch

Lay on the ground flat on your back with your arms extended. Keeping your upper body still cross one leg over the other, trying to touch the floor with your foot (see photo 12). Be careful not to bounce.

Bend and stretch

Grasp the edge of the bench keeping your legs slightly flexed. You can also use a the side of a golf cart for this warm-up. Flex your knees and stick your backside out until you feel a slight pulling in your back (see photo 13).

Strength training program

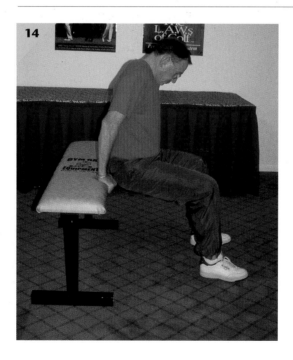

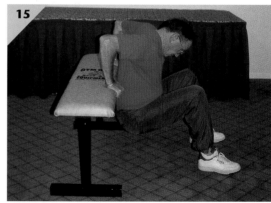

Triceps

This exercise works the extensor muscles that help you "sling" the club through impact. Using the bench, support your body with your arms, keeping your back straight (see photo 14). Lower your body by bending your arms (see photo 15), then raise it again by straightening your arms until they are fully extended. Do at least two sets of eight.

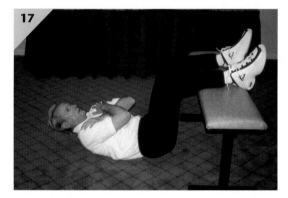

Crunches

This exercise works the abdominal muscles that stabilize your hips and back during the swing.

Lay on your back with your legs forming a 90-degree angle (see photo 16). Raise your shoulders off the ground and crunch your stomach muscles as you lift off (see photo 17).

Hamstrings

This exercise works the muscles on the back of your upper leg that curl the leg and allow you to keep your knee flex during the swing.

The hamstrings are very hard to work without special equipment, but this is the best substitute. Place your heels on the bench with your legs at a 90-degree angle and your shoulders flat on the floor (see photo 18). Lift your entire body by arching your back and pushing with your heels (see photo 19). Now lower yourself slowly back down. Do at least three sets of five reps.

Strength training program *continued*

Biceps curls

This exercise works the muscle that folds the arm and helps elevate and set the club during the swing. Start with a dumbbell at your side (photo 20), then, without moving your elbow, curl your hand to your shoulder (photo 21). Hold for a count and lower slowly. Alternate arms and do three sets of ten. Lifting too much weight at a certain angle (photo 22) ruins form and can cause injury.

Bench press

This exercise works the chest muscles that, among other actions, control the right arm in the down-swing. Lay on the bench with dumbbells over the edges of your shoulders, legs bent and heels on the bench (photo 23). Push your arms straight up (photo 24), then lower them. Do three sets of ten.

Lat saw

This works the back muscles that help return the club to the ball in the down-swing. Place your forehead on the back of a chair, using a towel as a cushion. Don't lock your knees (photo 25). Using your back muscles, not just your arms, bring the weight to your chest at an angle using a sawing motion (photo 26). Do three sets of ten and switch sides.

Forearm curls

This exercise works the forearm muscles that help grip the club. Sit on the bench and rest your right arm on your right thigh (see photo 27). Keeping your elbow anchored on your thigh, curl the weight toward your body at a slight angle. Do one set, then switch arms. Do three sets of ten for each arm. Then turn your right forearm over so that the palm is facing the floor (see photo 28) and repeat the above series.

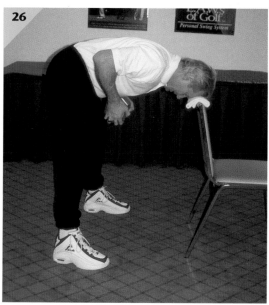

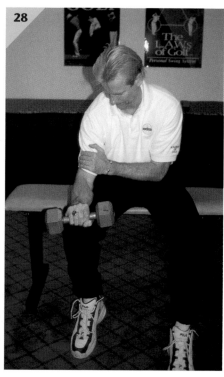

Strength training program *continued*

Squats

This exercise works the thigh and calf muscles that stabilize the lower body during your golf swing. Stand with your back straight and the weights at your side (photo 29).

Bend your knees to about 45 degrees (never go as far as 90) and keep your back straight as you lower the weights toward the ground (photo 30). Straighten your legs to lift the weights and raise yourself up until you are on your toes (photo 31).

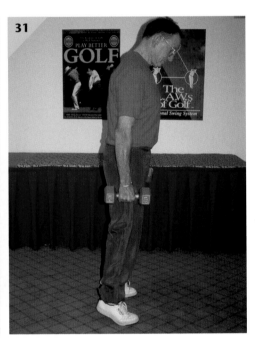

Athletic eyes

In his book *Sports Vision*, Dr. Leon Revien says, "Given proper training and conscious desire to carry out a specific physical task, one's visual ability can, indeed, be influenced and directed so that the body, in effect, can rise to the occasion, producing an accurate, fast, and coordinated response. In short, vision is learned and can be improved."

The eye, like any other structure, is controlled by muscles. The stronger those muscles are, the better you are going to be able to see. "If the muscles are functioning well and our eyes are correctly postured, the neural impulses from each eye are transmitted accurately through the optic nerve to the brain. The stimuli are then blended into a single three-dimensional image by a process known as fusion. When fusion is weak, it often means the ocular muscles are not coordinated and the wrong physical decision will be made."

Strong eye muscles prevent fatigue, increase your visual skills. In his book, Dr. Revien gives exercises for accommodation, acuity, convergence, peripheral vision, recognition, and most importantly for golfers, depth perception.

Depth perception

Pick out two objects a similar distance away from you, let's say one on either side of the fairway, at 250 yards or so. As you approach the two objects, study them intently to see if you can determine which one is actually closer to you. Repeat the process at different distances of perhaps 150 and 80 yards. Your brain can learn how to locate objects by using this kind of visual practice. It can also learn acuity, making your sighting of objects, like the flagstick, more clear and in focus. To sharpen the acuity of your vision, practice by making very precise observations of objects, such as reading car license numbers and road signs. On the golf course, perform similar exercises like reading what is written on the flag as soon as you are close enough.

One of the best exercises to strengthen the muscles of your eyes involves rotating your eyes without moving your head. This will exercise all of the muscles of your eyes. Your eyes should move together and at an even speed as they rotate in a circle, first counter-clockwise, then clockwise. Once the circle is completed ten times, reverse the direction.

Eye fatigue

Obviously, an important part of playing golf well is accurately locating the target, but with poor vision caused by eye fatigue, it is hard to process the visual information necessary to do so. To play your best golf you must have athletic eyes. You can build your eye muscles just like you would any muscles, and when they tire you can use palming to rejuvenate them.

Close your eyes and cover them with the palms of your hands. Apply very light pressure to the eye, and gently rotate your palms while maintaining the light pressure. Breathe deeply in and out and relax your body. Stop for a few seconds and repeat the massage at least twice. Take care though. Don't rub your eyes as if you had an itch, and be very careful not to push your palms into your eyes. Do not use palming at all if you wear contact lenses.

Eye fatigue can cause your facial muscles to tense and this tension can seep into the rest of your body. Though it is a low level tension you may not even be aware of, its prolonged effect can lead to exhaustion late in the round. To avoid this, consciously relax the muscles in your face from time to time, especially your jaw muscles, by letting your mouth hang open for about ten to 30 seconds. Breathe through your mouth and take air deep into your abdominal cavity, then exhale slowly. This combination of relaxed facial muscles and deep breathing decreases overall tension and helps conserve energy for those final holes.

Tension
buster

You can relax your eyes as well as your whole body in the following way: sit in your golf cart, or on a bench, and rest your head between your knees. If you are not flexible enough to do so, rest your head in your hands with your elbows on your knees and lower your arms as much as possible. Close your eyes and relax. Hold this position for about 60 seconds. This allows fresh, oxygenated blood to flow to the muscles of your eyes, increasing circulation.

Chapter nine

Healthy choices

Golf: it's the game of a lifetime

Most of the golfers on the PGA Senior Tour say they are playing better now than when they played on the regular tour. Many look

fit and are still playing well and winning money into their sixties and seventies. The Senior Tour players have found a way to not

Senior PGA Tour player Bruce Crampton is known as the 'Iron Man' for his physical fitness. only ward off the ravages of time, but to actually improve their skills. By matching their equipment and swing mechanics to what their bodies allow them to do, their athletic ability shines through. These players are accomplishing their goals in ways unheard of 40 years ago. They are taking care of themselves by using special, golf-specific, exercise programs and making other healthy choices, such as watching what they eat and drink and making sure they limit their exposure to the sun.

If the Senior Tour players can improve their games by making swing adjustments and keeping their bodies fit for golf, so can you.

Controlling exposure

There's nothing more invigorating then being outside on a sunny day. Studies show that people denied access to the sun for long periods of time can develop a sun deprivation syndrome called Seasonal Affective Disorder or SAD. But too much sun can cause a range of damage – from wrinkling your skin and dimming your eyesight to cancer. As Shaun Hughes, President of Sun Precautions, Inc., says, "The sun doesn't come with a warning label – but it should."

Protecting yourself from the sun's harmful effects can be difficult because most of the fabrics you wear when you play golf allow the sun to penetrate to the skin. Studies from the American Cancer Society show that the average golf shirt, especially when dampened with perspiration, lets in so much sun that it is almost like wearing no shirt at all. This is a prime reason why so many lesions grow on and must be removed from "covered" areas like the back and chest. Here are some ways to protect yourself while you enjoy a sun-splashed day on the golf course:

■ Use a sunscreen with a sun protection factor (SPF) of at least 15. Follow the manufacturer's instructions carefully.

■ Re-apply the sunscreen at least once during a round. A stick applicator form of sunscreen is the best for keeping your hands from getting greasy when you do so.

■ Use a sunscreen that gives both UVA and UVB protection.

■ Use a sunscreen that carries the Sun Cancer Foundation or similar seal of approval.

■ Avoid exposure to the sun, especially between the hours of 10 a.m. and 2 p.m.

■ Use an umbrella to shield yourself from long exposures.

■ Always wear a hat, preferably one with a wide brim to protect both face and neck.

■ Wear sunglasses designed to protect your eyes from UVA and UVB rays. Check the label for this if you are buying a new pair.

■ Wear special sun protective clothing such as the Solumbra line, from Sun Precautions, Inc of Arizona. Because of its effective sun protection, it is regulated as a medical device.

■ Don't be fooled by cloudy days – especially if you are fair skinned. Clouds don't block all the ultraviolet rays, so you still need protection.

A long-sleeved shirt, a hat, and sunglasses – essential equipment for a health-conscious golfer.

A game improvement strategy

The quality of your game depends not only on your golf swing but also on how you handle your water! Not the kind of water you have to hit a 3-wood over to get to the green, but the kind you need to drink to be healthy enough to hit that shot and every other shot correctly.

Muscle is 70 percent water, so you need to replace the fluid that you lose through perspiration to give your muscles the water they need to function. Your cells are little factories that produce heat when they are worked. Water helps release that heat from your body so you don't burn up your tissues. The water in perspiration cools the skin as it evaporates and this helps maintain the correct body temperature.

If you have ever seen pictures of the pioneers who settled the American West, you may have wondered why they were wearing long johns in the sweltering heat of the Great Plains. In fact, as their sweat soaked into the long johns, it set up a day-long evaporative cooling process that was highly efficient. This is why, if you are playing in really hot weather, it is not a good idea to change into a dry shirt for the back nine – it retards the sweating/cooling process.

When you don't drink enough water

When you run low on water, the body's various regulating systems become imbalanced – you don't see as well, your breathing changes and you will often become confused and irritable. Other symptoms of dehydration include a dry mouth and dry skin, weakness and fatigue, instability, dizziness, loss of balance, and a drop in blood pressure that reduces circulation and hampers your athletic performance. You can easily imagine the devastating effect even a mild form of these conditions can have on your golf game. A three-putt or a ball hit out of bounds are likely results. To complicate matters the dehydrated golfer is also likely to be short tempered, and will lose concentration and make irrational choices that cause scores to skyrocket.

The effects of dehydration don't just ruin your day, they can ruin your night as well. After the round you will be exhausted and, of course, extremely thirsty. You may crave sweets in the evening, and some authorities think those attention grabbing night cramps many people are troubled by are aggravated by the electrolyte disturbances that accompany dehydration.

As a golfer, playing a low exertion sport, you may not think that dehydration is much of a problem. Granted, you don't see dehydrated golfers with puffy, parched lips crawling on hands and knees to the water cooler. But that is just the point: dehydration is an insidious process. In its first stages – as encountered on the golf course – it may not cause you to stagger wildly, but you might lose your balance on a crucial drive, or mis-read a putt because your eyesight isn't as keen as it should be. Further more, the older you are, the easier it is to become dehydrated.

Dehydration also creates a dangerous cycle for the golfer: hit a few bad shots and the stress begins to build. Then, because your body uses up water more rapidly when you are stressed, your need for water increases.

The worst part of the problem is that, by the time you feel thirsty, the symptoms of dehydration will have already taken hold. Since water is so important to the body, you would think that the body would give an advanced warning and make you thirsty sooner. Instead, it is a fact that thirst is a poor indicator of your body's need for wate. Your strategy must be to drink water whether or not you feel thirsty. Here is your strategy:

■ Don't wait until you feel thirsty. Drink at least eight ounces (a large glass or mug) of water per hour every day. If you do feel thirsty on the course, drink twice as much water as it takes to quench your thirst.

■ Never drink sugary drinks like colas and lemonade while you play.

■ Make drinking water a part of your post-shot routine (see "Swing and swig" on p138).

■ Never drink alcohol or caffeine just before or while you play. If you must drink coffee before you play, drink two large glasses of water for every cup of coffee.

■ Drink small amounts of water frequently. If you wait for the beverage cart or the clubhouse at the turn and then gulp large amounts of water, it can lead to frequent urination and headaches.

■ Don't take salt pills; they make things worse. Putting a large concentration of salt in your stomach forces your system to draw water from the rest of your body to redress the imbalance by diluting the concentration of salt. This depletes the water supply available to other areas of the body, aggravating the dehydration.

■ Try not to drink from water coolers on the course.

Beware of the water coolers

At many golf courses, there are water coolers at stations out on the course. They are often filled from a hose and, although the water is most likely treated, it may not be up to the standard of cleanliness of the water you are used to drinking at home. The condition of the actual water coolers themselves may be a risk as well. Often, they are merely rinsed at the start of each day and re-filled. But, if the water in the cooler from the previous day got heated up, this could leave the container laden with bacteria. For this reason also, it is even more important to avoid coolers towards the end of a long hot day.

Drinking from a course-side water cooler is a common practice that we suggest you avoid.

A game improvement strategy *continued*

Swing and swig

The best way to assure a constant supply of fresh water on the course is to bring your own. Keeping it cool can be a problem, but not if you know the "freeze and squeeze" method. Buy several one-liter containers of bottled water. Empty one half of each bottle into another container for storage in the refrigerator and put the half-empty bottles in the freezer. Your only problem here is your memory, you may have to remind yourself to do this.

Just before you go to the course, take the now-frozen bottles from the freezer and fill them up with the water you stored in the refrigerator. Now you have a supply of fresh, ice-cold water that will keep cool for some time. To stop the ice from thawing too quickly you can also buy various types of insulating cover, some of which you pre-chill in your freezer. If you do not have any of these, the head-cover from one of your woods can be used as a substitute. Just slide the bottle inside.

Once you are on the course, make a habit of taking a swig of water after every full swing. After your round, clean and re-fill the bottles half-way as before and put them back in the freezer. It is a simple chore that pays major benefits. For the sake of your health, make the freeze and squeeze as much a part of your golf equipment as your clubs and your spikes.

Protect your hands

Golf becomes almost an impossible game if the joints in your hands and arms are aching. There is a simple but functional aid that can be added to your clubs to avoid the painful vibrations of mis-hits. Specially designed inserts fit into the shaft and dampen the vibrations that you would normally feel if you struck the ball badly. The effect of these vibrations can build over time, injuring your joints and irritating arthritis. There are currently three inserts available and approved by the USGA, and soon to be more. The

The simplest way to improve your game is to drink water regularly in the course of a round – whether you think you need to or not. This is one golf tip that you can start with tomorrow and get right every time without any practice.

If you mis-hit the ball you'll feel the vibration through impact.

Cushman Selective Filtering Insert is used in many Ping iron shafts and it looks like three tiny ball bearings in a protective casing. True Temper, a manufacturer of club shafts, offers Sensi-core inserts in many of its designs. In 1997, Davis Love became the first player to win a major championship – the PGA – using this technology. PowerBilt uses the Shock Relief Insert. The developer of this device, Steven Sims, has successfully introduced the insert to graphite irons and woods.

Nature's candy

The source of energy used for muscle contraction is carbohydrate, which is brought to the muscle through its blood supply as glucose. The glucose is stored in the muscle as a related product called glycogen, to be converted back into glucose as the muscle requires it for energy. If you feel tired in the middle of a round, it may be because of a depletion of this energy source and the build up of the by-products of the metabolic process, including lactic acid. If you are feeling a little grumpy or even a bit faint, you probably have a temporary case of low blood sugar (hypoglycemia). Carry an apple, a banana or a batch of "nature's candy" – raisins – with you when you play or practice. You could also try packing a "Geiberger burger," the peanut butter sandwich that the great Al Geiberger always had on hand.

To keep your energy levels high through-

A healthy snack during a round can work wonders for your game.

out your round, you'll do well if you stick to some simple, common sense rules regarding your diet. These rules will contribute to general good health as well as golfing success:

- Eat only when you are hungry.
- Eat small portions – big meals make you tired.
- Avoid fad diets.
- Always eat breakfast.
- Avoid fried and fat-laden food.
- Eat a balanced diet, with plenty of fresh fruits and vegetables.
- Eat a small meal at dinner and try to eat at least three hours before you go to bed.

Chapter ten

Strategy and course management

Strategy begins with practice

As you get older, an excellent way to maintain your skill level is to use your practice time more efficiently. To do so, keep a journal of the rounds you play where you evaluate your strengths and weaknesses, and dedicate your practice time to working on your weaknesses. This way, you spend your practice time making specific preparations for your next round of golf.

Building the fundamentals

You should constantly evaluate your game to determine what skills you should practice and what fundamentals need polishing. When you are working on fundamental swing elements, focus on what your body is doing, not what the ball is doing. Also, when you're practising the fundamentals, always set up a practice station with alignment clubs so you know you are aiming correctly (see sidebar). Good aim is the most basic element of golf, but one that is often neglected and rarely done correctly. Alignment clubs also help you confirm that your set-up is perfect, eliminating the possibility of many errors before they have the chance to occur.

To ingrain swing fundamentals, it also helps to do drills and use teaching aids. Teaching

aids and drills help you to experience correct sensations and remember them more easily. Though hard work with drills and teaching aids will lead to good habits, you need to wean yourself off them as soon as possible and create the movements on your own. The goal is to improve your golf swing, not to become proficient at doing drills or hitting balls with training aids in place. Once you begin to hit the ball better, it is time to work on target practice. A good rule of thumb is to alternate: hit five balls using the drill or aid and five without, until you don't need it any more.

Senior PGA Tour player Jim Albus practices putting to prepare for a round at the Senior PGA Championship.

Always "build" a hitting station like this when you practice.

Strategy begins with practice *continued*

Target Practice

Target practice allows for an easy transition from the driving range to the first tee.

Golf is a target game, but many golfers forget to aim at a target when they hit balls on the range. When working on target practice, your focus must shift away from swing mechanics and be solely on the target. And you need to let your brain know that this is exactly what you want to do on the course. So, when you work on target practice, you should always do so as if you were "playing," and go through your entire pre-shot routine for every shot. It is also a good idea to hit your shots to a specific target on the driving range, varying the target so you are actually simulating the game of golf. For example, hit a driver, then an 8-iron, then a 20-yard pitch.

Develop this practice routine to allow an easy transition from the driving range to the first tee. Here's how to do it. When you work on target practice, visualize playing your favorite golf course or the course you will play on for your next round of golf. Take whichever club you would normally hit off the first tee and visualize the hole in your mind. Use your imagination to overlay your mental picture of that hole onto your driving range. Prepare to hit your drive as you usually would by going through your complete pre-shot routine, and only then actually hit your shot.

Evaluate the quality of your opening "drive" and determine what club and type of shot you would consequently have to hit on the course you are visualizing. For example, if you have hit an exceptional drive, well down the center of the fairway, that would normally leave you an 8-iron to the green, visualize that approach shot and hit an 8-iron next. But if you mis-hit your tee shot, resulting in a loss of distance that would put you a 5-iron away from the green, visualize that shot and hit the 5-iron. When you "play" the golf course on the range, you are practicing playing the game, not the mechanics of your golf swing.

The scoring shots

Next you need to spend time on scoring shots from just off the green. While practicing your short game, the same principles apply. You will either be working on fundamental skills or a specific playing situation. Again, while working on fundamentals, your focus should be on correct mechanics; while working on playing situations, your focus should be on the target.

When working on fundamentals, use several balls so you can repeat the same shot from the same position and make your skill a habit. When you are working on play situations use one ball, dropping it in a different lie each time and executing the necessary shot to the

When working on fundamental building, repeat the same shot from the same position to make the skill a habit.

practice green. Whatever happens, take your putter and putt out. You can play 9 or 18 holes, setting a "par" of 2 for easy up-and-downs, and a "par" of 3 for more difficult positions.

Pre-round preparation

To prepare yourself for a round of golf, first choose the utility clubs you will need to match your game to the course you are playing. For example, on a short, tight, golf course with small greens, take your driver out of the bag and add a wedge. Your 3-wood will provide you sufficient distance off the tee and maximize your accuracy, making the driver unnecessary. Since the greens are small,

the extra wedge will help you get the ball up-and-down from those inevitable missed greens.

When you face a course with elevated greens, make sure you have a lofted sand-wedge (60 degrees or even 64 degrees of loft). If you have not already done so, take your long irons out of your bag in favor of lofted fairway woods (5-, 7-, 9-, or even 11-woods);

Pre-round preparation *continued*

Jack Nicklaus, a master of course strategy, often hit a 3-wood from the tee.

shots from these clubs fly higher and land softer on elevated greens.

If the course you are playing is long and wide open you might want to add a long-shafted driver for extra distance off the tee. If you normally use a long putter but you are playing a course with big greens, you might want to carry two putters. Adding a conventional length putter will let you perform better on the longer putts you will inevitably face.

The Rules of Golf limit a player to 14 clubs, so be sure that whenever you add a club, you take another out of your bag. Before the start of a competition, it is a good idea to count your clubs just before you go to the first tee to make sure you are not over the legal limit. Johnny Miller lost a tournament when his four-year-old son put his plastic toy putter in daddy's bag and, because it was so small, it wasn't noticed. Miller was penalized four shots and ever since, he has meticulously counted his clubs before he tees off – and so should you.

It is a good idea to arrive at the course at least an hour before your tee time. First work on the short-game shots you are going to need when you play. Then hit short, medium and long putts to get used to the speed of the greens. Finally warm up your full swing on the range and rehearse some of the key shots that you will be needing for this particular course.

While you are warming up, do not make the mistake of trying to give yourself a lesson. Just work on two things: balance and solid contact. First, to give your brain the idea of solid contact, tee the ball and choke down on a 7-iron. Make three-quarter swings and don't worry about how far the ball travels; your goal is solid contact. Once you have achieved this simple goal, tee up a 5-iron and then a few drivers, once again making solid contact, rather than distance, your goal. Second, for every warm-up shot, try to finish in perfect balance, no matter where the ball goes. Soon your brain will get the message that balance and solid contact are the order of the day.

The ABC strategy

A pre-round warm up is not the time to give yourself a lesson. It is the time to find your ABC strategy.

Evaluating
pin positions

Think of pin positions as red light, yellow light, and green light situations. If a pin is protected by two conditions, for example, if it is tucked beside a bunker, and the wind is blowing toward the bunker, consider it a red light situation and play to the center of the green. If the pin is more accessible, but is still protected by one condition, perhaps just the bunker, consider it a yellow light situation. When the pin is in an open area of the green, that's a green light pin. Use your ABC Strategy and plan your attack accordingly.

The ABC strategy *continued*

Regardless of handicap, every golfer has good days and bad, swing-wise. A key element in your pre-round preparation is to determine what "game" you have that day while you are warming up on the range. On the days when you are hitting the ball your best, you have your "A-game." Most of the time, when you are hitting the ball in a way that's standard for you, you have your "B-game." On those unfortunate days when you are hitting the ball your worst, you have your "C-game."

When you have your A-game and you are hitting the ball solidly and accurately, it is your day to be aggressive and attack the course. You will hit driver and 3-wood from the tee, and aim aggressive approach shots right at "yellow-light" or "green-light" pins (see sidebar).

More often you will have your B-game. Your shots may not be as solid. The ball flight may be curving, but consistently so, with all your shots fading from left to right, for example. Because a driver maximizes side spin, use a 3-wood or 5-wood from the tee on these days to reduce the effect of spin. Since you are not making the most solid of contacts, your ball will not travel your maximum distance, so use one more club on approach shots to the green. With your B-game, play to safe, open, areas of the green, taking aim only at "green-light" pins. The point of this style is to recognize the fact that you are going to miss more shots than

when you have your A-game: accept it and rely on your short game to carry you through.

Then there are those dreaded days when you arrive at the course and find you have your C-game: the ball is flying in every direction and almost every shot is a mis-hit. The first key is not to try to "fix" your swing five minutes before your tee time. Mechanical swing thoughts will just make the problem worse. Commit yourself to a conservative game plan. Hit a 5- or 7-wood, or even an iron, from the tee and aim at the widest landing area the fairway has to offer. This will probably mean you won't be able to reach the green in regulation, but your plan is to avoid a big score. When you are within striking distance of the green, ignore the pin position and aim for the safest area. This way, if you miss the green all together, you will be left with a relatively easy chip shot. This is not a negative approach, it is a realistic one. The ABC strategy lets you score well on those days when your game is a B or C.

The days you have your C-game will serve as the ultimate test of your course management and strategy skills. If you handle the opening holes with patience and stick to your conservative game plan, you may "find" your swing a few holes later and be right back to the comfort of your B-game. But if you make the mistake of playing aggressive golf when you are suffering with your C-game, you are in for a long day.

Sharpen your target awareness

Whether you have your A-, B- or C-game, you must focus on the target for every shot you play. For those who have been playing golf for many years, this advice is hardly revolutionary. Yet think back to the last round you played. Once you addressed the ball, was your mind invariably fixed on your target? Or were you thinking about the last putt you missed, the bunker on the left side of the fairway, the water on the right side of the green, and so on?

Staying focused on a target – even for the short time a golfer stands over the ball – requires a great deal of concentration, and is a skill you have to practice. To help your mind hold its focus, make your target as clear and distinct as possible. For example, when picking a landing area for your tee shot, "in the fairway" is not distinct. "The left center of the fairway" is better because the reference is more specific. But better still would be "the left center of the fairway, just to the right of the dark patch of grass, and on line with the lone pine tree in the distance." Obviously, there is an endless variety of circumstances, but the more specific you make each of your targets, the more easily you will hold the image in your mind and your ability to concentrate will automatically improve.

One of Golf's greatest champions, Lee Trevino is a master at hitting his targets.

Pre-shot routine

Intermediate
target

Since the rules of golf require players to stand beside the target line, instead of on it as in most target sports, aiming correctly can be a difficult task. An intermediate target can help. As you survey the target from behind the ball, choose an easily distinguishable mark or object on your intended target line about 5 to 10 feet in front of the ball. When you walk in to address the ball, this intermediate target will confirm the line you selected from the ideal vantage point behind the ball.

Having a good pre-shot routine is an essential element to keeping your focus on the target. A pre-shot routine is also an integral part of making a quality golf swing and, however personalized it is, no expert player is without one. A good routine calms you down because you make the same preparations, in the same order, for every shot you play. Once it becomes "routine," you can stand over the ball with confidence, knowing that all areas of preparation have been addressed. When you are under stress, the habitual rhythm of your routine protects you against the tendency to hurry or delay your shot. By developing a solid routine, you will insulate yourself from external distractions, like a cart passing on the adjacent hole, and be ready to pull the trigger with confidence.

Good golf shots are a combination of correct distance and direction but you will confuse your brain if you think about both details during your swing. One part of the pre-shot routine is to separate the two: you pick your target, aim the club-face, and align your body correctly. Having done so, all the requirements for direction are satisfied. The key is to trust your set-up and avoid any temptation to "steer" the ball with your swing.

The specifics of the pre-shot routine

Stand behind the ball and pick a specific target. Make sure your practice swing is a true rehearsal of the up-coming shot by making a swing in the direction of the target, off a similar lie, and at the same speed as the swing you are about to make. If you are hitting a driver from the tee, make sure you don't take a divot; if you are hitting an iron, make sure the club hits the ground. If you do the opposite in either case, you are rehearsing an error and are likely to repeat it. Once you have pictured the shot in your mind and made a practice swing, take a deep breath to relax.

Now step into your address position, with your right foot (for right-handers) leading the

1 A good pre-shot routine begins behind the ball.

way. Before you bring your left foot into position, sole the club-face behind the ball, with the leading edge perpendicular to the target line. Then, while keeping the club-head exactly as you have placed it, bring your left foot into position and drop your right foot back from the target line, as in the S swing. You

have now locked-in your direction.

From this position, take one look at the target by rotating your head without lifting it, waggle, and then swing. Each individual will have nuances to the routine. For instance, you may want to look at the target twice before you swing, which is fine. The

The waggle, the habitual movement of the hands or body just before you begin your swing, is an excellent way to relieve tension. It is the bridge between the somewhat static position of address and the active motion of your swing. You can make your waggle a miniature rehearsal for a good swing, if you know how. To do this, match your waggle to the motion you will be trying to make in the initial part of your swing. For example, if you know you tend to swing the club too far round behind you, waggle the club on a path straight back along the target line to prepare for the take-away you are trying to produce.

2 The second stage in the pre-shot routine is to step into the address position.

Pre-shot routine *continued*

3 When you look at your target from the address position always rotate your head. Do not distort your perception by lifting your head.

4 If you follow a good set-up routine you will be ready to swing without tension, with your thoughts fixed on the target.

important point here is to be consistent. If you normally look at the target twice, but then on one shot find yourself looking at the target a third or fourth time, your routine has

been broken. Treat this as a firm signal to step away, gather more information, perhaps switch clubs, and then step up to the ball with new-found confidence in your plan.

Club selection

When determining the right club for a particular shot, you have to consider not just the

Always make use of the information available from the yardage markers.

"real" yardage, but the "effective" yardage. A golf course is riddled with variables that affect the distance the ball travels. Wind, the lie of the ball, air temperature, humidity, differences in elevation between ball and target, the altitude of the place where you are playing, the pin position – all affect the distance the ball travels.

Yardage markers are provided on most courses to indicate the distance to the center of the green. So, the first step in calculating effective yardage is to consider the location of the pin. Most greens are at least 30 yards deep, so if the pin is in the back of the green, you need to add ten yards to your distance calculation; if it is in the front of the green, you need to subtract about ten yards.

To determine the effect of the wind, check the speed and direction the clouds are moving, look at the flag, and note any movement of the tops of the trees. The wind that you can actually feel where you are standing may not be at the same intensity for the flight of your shot. If you are playing against the wind, obviously you will take more club; downwind, less club. If you estimate the wind to be less than 5 miles per hour, you can ignore it. Since a cross wind pushes the ball away from the target, it will add to the effective distance of your shot too because, as your ball rides the wind, it will need to take a longer curved path to your target than if it flew straight.

When the ball is in the rough, with the grass growing toward the target, you have what's known as a "jumper lie." The ball will fly farther than usual because the grass acts as a launching pad for the shot. In this instance, take one less club than the yardage dictates. If, on the other hand, the grass is growing away from the target, it provides resistance to the club-head and the ball will fly a shorter distance.

When you are hitting uphill or downhill you will also need to adjust the real yardage. For every 30 feet of elevation change, add or subtract ten yards. When you are playing in high humidity expect the ball to fly a shorter distance. If you are playing at high altitude, the ball will fly farther.

When you can't reach the green

Occasionally the yardage of the hole exceeds your ability to reach the green in regulation. In this case, do not use your driver at the tee, especially if you are not accurate with it. Since the length of the hole puts you at a disadvantage before you even start, you don't need to complicate matters by hitting an errant drive into the trees. The smart strategy when you are faced with a long par-4 that is out of reach is to use a club off the tee that you can confidently hit in the fairway. You will need three shots to reach the green no matter what, so if you can make them extremely accurate, you may have an easy putt for par.

Always think of the direction in which the grass is growing when your ball is in the rough.

Follow the architect's plan

Senior PGA Tour player Tom Wargo hitting a tee shot.

Every golf hole has an ideal landing area for a tee shot, the place from where the course designer gives you the easiest approach to the green. If you have the opportunity, walk your home course backwards, from the greens to the tees. From this perspective you will see how each hole was designed to be played, and the ideal landing areas for your tee shots that offer the best angles of approach to the greens. On a well-designed hole, the widest and safest landing area will usually be beside a "bail out area" – an area off the fairway that is not ideal, but is not as troublesome as the steep-faced bunkers or deep rough there may be elsewhere. This will help you plan your strategy for the round.

Strategy hole-by-hole

Par-3s

Par-3s are the shortest holes on the course, but this should not make you assume they are easy. Par-3s actually provide some of the game's great challenges. They are usually defended by more bunkers than other greens, so be sure to evaluate your bunker skills when making your plan. If you have a yellow light pin guarded by a bunker, but

On this par-3 the top priority with the tee shot is keeping it out of the water.

The challenge on this par-4 is to work out the correct placement of your tee shot, avoiding trouble but leaving a good line of approach to the green.

your sand play needs work, aim your shot to a part of the green left unprotected by bunkers. This becomes your target, not the flag. If the bunkers are in the front of the green, take an extra club and plan to land the ball on the back. This way, you will be sure to carry the bunkers, and if you miss the green long, at least you won't be in the sand. If water guards the front of the green, once again take an extra club and focus on a target at the back of the green, not necessarily the flag.

Par-4's

Architects guard par-4s with length and hazards. Therefore, on a well-designed short par-4 where the challenge of length is removed, you can be sure trouble awaits,

Using a tee on a par three?

Always use a tee when you start a hole, even with a short iron. If you choose to hit the ball off the ground, there is an increased chance of hitting it "fat", producing a shorter shot than you planned. Also, when your ball is on the ground, it is common to catch some grass between the club-face and ball. This lowers backspin and causes the ball to roll more when it lands, going farther than intended. Since par-3s are accuracy holes, ensure that you get the true distance from the club you choose: tee the ball every time so you are more likely to make solid contact.

Strategy hole-by-hole *continued*

even if you can't always see it from the tee. In this case, think carefully before you choose to hit a driver. But do not be too conservative in your club selection. You do not want to leave yourself a long approach shot, because short holes usually feature small greens built to accept the high trajectory of a short iron. Small greens need to be approached with higher shots allowing the ball to land softly and stop quickly.

If it is possible to see the green from the tee, observe the location of the flag so you can favor the side of the fairway that gives you the best angle for your approach shot. You may be able to see and make a mental note of where a hidden flag is positioned while you are playing an earlier hole on the course. On a dog-leg hole, so named for its resemblance to the angled shape of a dog's hind leg, be especially careful to hit the correct side of the fairway from the tee. On a dog-leg that bends from left to right, for example, you might not have a clear shot to the green if you land your drive on the right side of the fairway.

When a par-4 requires a long approach shot, most of the trouble will usually be left and right, to catch off-line shots. Thankfully, though, long par-4s usually make a feature of having large greens that are receptive to longer shots, so take plenty of club and make a smooth swing. If you have a favorite "straight" club (say a 7- or 5-wood) use it to stay out of the trouble on the left and right of the green.

When you are faced with an especially long par-4 that is well out of your reach in regulation, treat it as a par-5 and play to your strength. For example, if you struggle with 30-yard pitch shots and feel more comfortable with a full shot from around 100 yards, don't hit a driver and then a 3-wood if that positions you at the awkward 30-yard distance. Instead use a 3-wood from the tee, then say a 7-wood to leave the distance you prefer. This way, you can hit an approach shot you are more comfortable with.

The logic of proper course management says that if you can't reach the green in two shots (or in regulation on any hole), choose more accurate clubs for your first and second shots, leaving you an approach shot with a club you know you can knock close to the hole. The key with the long par-4s is to avoid score-wrecking disasters. These almost inevitably occur when you are trying to reach every par-4 in two simply because you are "supposed to."

Par-5s

Theoretically, par-5s are the hardest holes because they are the longest, forcing amateurs to take the most swings and thus increasing the chances of a mistake. But for those who hit the ball long and straight, par-5s

can be the easiest holes.

Architects tend to design trouble on par-5s to test long hitters who try to reach the green in two shots rather than the regulation three. If you go for a par-5 in two, trouble almost certainly awaits a mis-hit or mis-directed second shot to the green. If you therefore decide to play the hole conservatively in the standard three shots, once again make sure you play to your own particular strengths. Keep the odds in your favor by making wise club selections.

A typical par-5 may test longer hitters with a daunting carry over water if they try to reach the green in two.

155

GLOSSARY

19th hole

Golf slang for the bar in the clubhouse; for many, the next stop after completion of the 18th hole.

90 degree rule

A golf cart rule that directs players to keep their carts on the cart path except to enter and exit the fairway at a 90-degree angle to where their ball has come to rest.

Approach shot

Your first attempt at hitting your ball to a green on a par four or five.

Away

The player whose ball is furthest "away" from the hole plays first. "It's your turn" and "You're away" have the same meaning in golf.

Bag drop

When you arrive at the golf course, you can leave your clubs at the "bag drop" and then park your car. This avoids carrying your clubs from the parking lot.

Balloon

A shot hit into a strong wind loses its forward motion as the wind carries it high into the air.

Birdie

One shot less than par on any given hole.

Bogey

One shot more than par on any given hole.

Bunker

A depression on the course filled with sand or covered with grass.

Caddie

Though few courses offer this option, a caddie carries your clubs so you can walk as you play. A caddie is often knowledgeable about the course and can assist you with course management.

Carry

How far your ball travels on the fly. When you have to hit your ball a certain distance to "carry" over a hazard or onto the green, you'll want to know how far each of your clubs "carries" in the air or how far you need to "carry" your shot to clear the hazard.

Cart path only

A rule, established at the discretion of each facility, that prohibits golf carts from being driven anywhere other than on the cart path.

Chip

A low running shot played from within about five yards from the green (compare to *Pitch*).

Coil

In golf, coil is the ratio between how much your shoulders out-turn your hips and legs in your backswing. Building coil is the purpose of your backswing, because it is the unleashing of this coil into the ball that produces distance.

Compression

A term associated with golf balls. Manufacturers rate their balls based on how hard or easily they are compressed at impact. If your swing speed is low or the weather is cold, you may want a low- compression ball for a softer feel. The ratings are 80, 90, and 100, where 80 is the most easily compressed. There is, however, no significant relation between compression and distance.

Custom fitting/ custom clubs

In order to have custom clubs made, a fitter observes your swing and adjusts a range of specifications outlined in the equipment chapter. True custom fitting can only be accomplished by hitting golf balls in the presence of the fitter. Custom club maker Pat Lange of Lange Golf says, "There are five specific factors we address in our fitting system: club head selection, shaft selection, length, grip size, and lie. Unless each of these factors has been addressed, you haven't been fitted."

Cross wind

A wind that blows across the intended line of flight of your golf ball.

Dog leg

Refers to the shape of some golf holes, so named for their resemblance to a dog's hind leg. These holes bend from left to right or right to left.

Dormie

In matchplay you are said to be "dormie" when you lead by the same number of holes that are left to be played. You'll be dormie when you're three up with three holes to play.

Driver

The object off a par four and five is to hit or drive your ball down the fairway. The club of choice is often a one wood, most commonly referred to as a driver. It should hit the ball the furthest of all the clubs in your bag.

Drop zone

Drop zones are marked areas on the course where you can take relief from certain situations, such as ground under repair, wet areas, or temporary immovable obstructions. At some courses, where there are long, forced carries, drop areas are available, at your option, when your shot doesn't clear the water hazard. Often they are located closer to the hole, so that the length of the carry is diminished.

Eagle

Two strokes less than par.

Etiquette

Commonly thought of as the first rule of golf, etiquette concerns itself with consideration for your fellow golfers and the golf course itself.

Fat

Hitting the ground before you hit the ball. Also known as heavy. "I hit that ball a little fat/heavy."

Flagstick

The hole in the putting green is marked by a pole and flag anchored in its center known as the flagstick, more loosely referred to as the pin or flag.

Fore

A warning call to other golfers that an errant shot is about to hit them.

Foursome

Golf is most often played in groups of four, known as a foursome; groups of two or three are referred to as twosomes and threesomes.

Gimmie

On the putting green, a ball that comes to rest within a few inches of the hole is said to be a "gimmie" because in matchplay your competitor can concede you these putts. Gimmie range varies depending on the players involved and the situation of the match. A putt cannot be conceded in strokeplay.

Grain

The direction the grass grows on a putting surface, which can affect the direction your ball rolls. When the grass lies in such a way that it points toward the hole it's called down grain and your putt will be faster than

normal. If the grass grows away from the hole, your putt is into the grain and it will be slower.

Greenie

Slang for hitting the green in regulation and being closest to the pin.

Group

You and the golfers you are playing with are said to be a group. "The group on the third hole is playing extremely slowly."

Handicap

Though tournament handicaps are computed with a complicated formula, for a general guide your handicap is the number of strokes your average score is over par.

Hazard

This term is strictly defined in the Rules of Golf, but, generally speaking, it is an obstacle of water or sand on a golf course.

Heavy

See *Fat*.

Hold the green

A shot that stays on the green is said to have held the green. "I hit that ball too low and it couldn't hold the green."

Hole

The goal of golf is to get your ball in the hole in as few shots as possible; it's also referred to as the cup.

Hole in one

When you hit your ball from the tee and it goes in the hole you've made a hole in one. Although a rarity, it usually happens on a par three.

GLOSSARY

Inside the leather

In golf lingo, a ball that comes to rest within an area no greater than the length of your putter's grip is said to be inside the leather (of your grip). Casually speaking, these putts are said to be "gimmies" (see *Gimmie*).

Irons

The irons, which refer to the material they are most often made from, produce progressively more height and less length, e.g. a nine iron goes much higher and shorter than a four iron. Used for the accuracy required to hit and "hold" greens.

Jail

When your ball comes to rest behind a stand of trees or other blockades, then you have put yourself in jail.

Jumper lie

In the rough, when the grass grows in the direction you intend to hit your ball, the ball "jumps" off the club face and travels a greater distance than normal.

Landing area

The ideal spot to land your ball in the fairway.

Lie angle

The angle the shaft creates with the ground as measured from the mid point of the shaft.

Lift, clean, and place

Under certain conditions, The Rules of Golf and/or local rules allow you to lift, clean, and place your ball back on the grass. Normally, the ball is played as it lies and you are prohibited from touching it until it comes to rest on the green, but if the course is extremely wet, this rule may be put into effect.

Local rules

In addition to the Rules of Golf, sometimes there are additional rules based on idiosyncrasies of their course.

Loft

The angle your club face forms with the ground, i.e. how much the face of your club looks at the sky.

Match

Matchplay is where you play against a competitor and either win, lose or tie (known as halve) each hole played until the match is decided. For every hole you win, you are "one up" and for every hole you lose you are "one down." When you win the match on the seventeenth hole, it's called "two and one", i.e. you're two up with only one hole to play. If you lost the match on the twelfth hole, you've lost seven and six—seven down with six holes to play.

Medal

In medal competitions the lowest score wins and the winner is deemed the "medalist." This form of play is also commonly known as stroke play.

Metal wood

Woods were originally so named because their heads were crafted from wood. Now they are more often made of metal or other materials, and are referred to as "metal woods."

Par

The number of shots required by an expert to complete a hole. The total of all the pars gives the "course par," e.g. "it's a par 72" layout.

Pin

See *Flagstick*.

Pitch

A lofted shot played from an area around the green (compare to *Chip*).

Play it as it lies

Under the Rules of Golf, you are obliged to play the ball as it has come to rest on the course (compare to *Lift, clean, and place*).

Play through

If the group of golfers ahead of you is playing too slowly they may ask you to "play through" which means they will stand aside and let you play the hole, then resume play. The pace of play at most courses is designed for foursomes so if the course is crowded and you're playing in a twosome or onesome (by yourself) don't expect to be asked to play through.

Preferred lies

Also known as "winter rules," preferred lies indicate that you can roll the ball onto a better lie in the fairway. This is against the Rules of Golf but is often used in casual competition when the condition of the fairways is poor. If you answer "yes" to the question "Are we rolling them today?" you're playing preferred lies.

Release

During the backswing an important angle of power is created between the left arm and the club shaft. Once this 90-degree angle is made it must be released just before impact so that the club and ball meet with solid contact. If you hold this angle for too long or let it go too early, you've ruined your release and you won't hit the ball as far as you should.

Recovery shot

If you hit your shot into trouble and get yourself out of this bad situation you are said to have hit a nice "recovery shot."

Royal & Ancient Golf Club of St. Andrews

This organization, in conjunction with the United States Golf Association, has established The Rules of Golf. It is casually referred to as the "R & A."

Rub of the green

When your ball takes an unfair bounce it's known as the run of the green or, more commonly, as a bad luck.

Sand save

When your approach shot misses the green and lands in a bunker, you'll make what's known as "sand save" when you hit your ball from the bunker onto the green and sink the putt for a par. Also known as a "sandie" or a good "up and down."

Shaft flex

During the swing, the shaft of a properly fit club flexes from side to side and bows downward. This is intensified during the downswing where the shaft kicks into the ball at impact. Shafts come in various flexes. Too stiff a shaft causes a loss of distance and a low trajectory. You should swing the most flexible shaft you can handle.

Side wind

See *Cross wind*.

Sky ball

See *Pop up*.

Snowman

When you make a score of eight on a hole it's known as a "snowman" due to the number's resemblance to a snowman.

Starter

Before you begin your round of golf, many courses have you check in with an employee known as the starter. This person makes sure you have paid the appropriate fees, advises you of local rules and makes sure you tee off at the proper time.

Static fit

Trying to fit clubs without the client hitting golf balls.

Stroke

1   An upper body motion used for putting and chipping.
2   The point system in golf: each time you hit a ball it counts as a stroke. Your total number of strokes is your score.

Stroke play

See *Medal*.

Sweet spot

The ideal contact point on the face of every club: woods, iron and putter. The sweet spot is the perfectly balanced center of the club face which produces the most solid contact with minimal turning or twisting at impact.

Target line

An imaginary line extending from your ball to your target.

Tee shot

The shot you hit from the teeing ground of any golf hole.

Tee time

A reservation for a round of golf.

Thin

When the leading edge makes contact too high on the back edge of the golf ball you've hit what's known as a "thin shot" (compare to *Fat*).

Trajectory

Depending on what club you choose, a well-hit golf shot travels on different trajectories because of the loft of each club. Trajectory is the up and down curve of your golf ball.

Trap

Slang term for a sand bunker. You won't find the word "trap" in the rule book; it's a bunker, either sand or grass.

USGA

The United States Golf Association, in conjunction with the Royal & Ancient Golf Club of St. Andrews, has established The Rules of Golf. Casually referred to as the "USGA."

Whippy

A shaft that is too flexible for the golfer swinging it. A whippy shaft bows and bends excessively during the swing and causes a wild shot pattern—some left, some right, and some hooks mixed with slices.

Winter rules

See *Preferred lies*.